INDIGENOUS PEOPLE AND POLITICS

Edited by
David Wilkins
University of Minnesota
Franke Wilmer
Montana State University

A ROUTLEDGE SERIES

INDIGENOUS PEOPLE AND POLITICS
DAVID WILKINS AND FRANKE WILMER, *General Editors*

INVENTING INDIGENOUS KNOWLEDGE
Archaeology, Rural Development, and
the Raised Field Rehabilitation Project
in Bolivia
Lynn Swartley

The Globalization of Contentious Politics
The Amazonian Indigenous Rights Movement

Pamela L. Martin

Routledge
New York & London

Published in 2003 by
Routledge
29 West 35th Street
New York, NY 10001
www.routledge-ny.com

Published in Great Britain by
Routledge
11 New Fetter Lane
London EC4P 4EE
www.routledge.co.uk

Routledge is an imprint of the Taylor & Francis Group
Printed in the United States of America on acid-free paper.

10 9 8 7 6 5 4 3 2 1

Library of Congress Cataloging-in-Publication Data
Martin, Pamela
  Globalization of contentious politics : the Amazonian indigenous rights movement /
Pamela Martin.
      p. cm. — (Indigenous people and politics)
  Includes bibliographical references and index.
  ISBN 0-415-94426-0
  1. Indians of South America—Ecuador—Politics and government. 2. Indians of
South America—Ecuador—Government relations. 3. Indigenous peoples—Politics
and government. 4. Social movements—Ecuador. 5. Human rights—International
cooperation. I. Title. II. Series.
F3721.3.P74 M37 2003
323.1'980866—dc21   2002068255

Contents

Acknowledgments

THIS RESEARCH PROJECT IS A COMBINATION OF THE EFFORT AND SUPPORT OF many persons and institutions. I would like to thank the Institute for the Study of World Politics for granting me a doctoral dissertation fellowship, which provided me the resources and time needed to complete the fieldwork portion of the project. A grant from the Latin American Studies Program from the University of Maryland, College Park also aided me in attending a Fulbright-sponsored summer course on Quichua. Dr. Carmen Chuquín, Dr. Frank Salomon, and Dr. Lynn Meisch welcomed me to Ecuador and inspired me to learn more about Quichua peoples and culture. La Universidad Andina sponsored my stay in Ecuador the first year of my research and provided me with an excellent research facility. I particularly thank Raúl Vallejo, Fernando Balseca, and Dr. Enrique Ayala Mora for their support of my project and their hospitality. Thank you, Raúl, for sparking my interest in your country. La Universidad San Francisco de Quito also provided me with a Teaching Fellowship my second year in Ecuador. I would like to thank Dr. Luís Antonio Aguilar Monsalve, Dr. Raúl Carrera, Dr. José Julio Cisneros, Dr. Santiago Gangotena, Dr. Carlos Montúfar, and Dr. Diego Quiroga for their suggestions to my research project, the opportunity to teach in such a wonderful environment, and for their friendships. La Facultad Latinoaméricano de Ciencias Sociales (FLACSO) also provided me with support during my research, particularly Dr. Adrián Bonilla. I would also like to thank Ariruma Kowii, Professor of Quichua, in La Universidad Salesiana, Quito, Ecuador for helping me establish my first contacts with the Ecuadorian indigenous confederations and for his friendship.

My research for this project began at the University of Maryland, College Park. I would like to thank the Department of Government and Politics for its support of my project through a Graduate Fellowship during my doctoral program. Many professors have contributed to my ideas in some form, however a few stand out as special in that formation. Thank you to Dr. Ollie Johnson for making me care about "race" and "ethnicity" and for always having time to talk with me. Thank you to Dr. Ken Conca for making me question my ideas about the "Third World" and for your invaluable advice on field work in South America. *Dioselopagui* (thank you) to Dr. Regina Harrison for opening my eyes to the Quichua language and culture. You have been a constant friend as well as inspiration. Dr. Virginia Haufler, a model to all women in the discipline, not only inspired my ideas on International Political Economy, but always knew exactly what to say or do to aid me in times of crisis—I can not thank you enough. Dr. Ted Robert Gurr, my disseration chair, suggested a study of Ecuador and Mexico in 1994 during his seminar on "Civil Conflict." He spent many long hours talking to me about transnational actors in this process and has guided my professional development over the past four years. Even when the process seemed too long and arduous, Dr. Gurr always sent kind messages of motivation and support. I have appreciated so much this guidance and encouragement over the years and distances. I would also like to thank Ms. Ann Marie Clark for her constant administrative aid—many times at the last minute—and without a word of complaint.

Finally, I would like to express my deep gratitude and love for my friends and family who have endured this process with me. First, I thank my parents, Jeanne and Arthur Burke for always being by my side—even when my plans sounded questionable. Much love and thanks to my grandmother, Margaret Jednesty for taking the time to read my chapters. Dr. Michael Cataldo and Mrs. Marilyn Cataldo are the most wonderful uncle and aunt that anyone could ask for and I appreciate all of their words of advice and encouragement. Dr. Valentina Padula has been a source of constant friendship and inspiration whenever I needed it. Elvira Vallejo, Rita Loreto, and María José Sevilla have been good friends and made me feel like I have family in Ecuador. Last, but certainly not least, I thank my husband, Bill Martin, for bringing so much joy and happiness to my life, and for always supporting my adventures and passions.

Abbreviations

ACT	Amazonian Cooperation Treaty
ARCO	ARCO Oil Company
BIC	Bank Information Center
CEDIME	Center of Documentation and Information of Social Movements
CEDR	Center for Environmental Design Research of the University of California
CEPE	Ecuadorian State Petroleum Corporation
CESR	Center for Economic and Social Rights
CIEI	Center for the Study of Indigenous Education
Coalition	The Coalition for Amazonian Peoples and their Environment
COICA	Coordinator of Indigenous Organizations in the Amazon Basin
COICE	Coordinator of Indigenous Organizations of the Coast of Ecuador
CONACNIE	Coordinating Council of Indigenous Nationalities of Ecuador
CONAIE	Confederation of Indigenous Nationalities of Ecuador
CONFEIAE	Confederation of Indigenous Nationalities of the Ecuadorian Amazon
CORDAVI	Confederation of Lawyers for the Environment in

Ecauador

DIGEMA	General Directorate on the Environment
ECUARUNARI	Ecuador Runacunapac Riccharimui - Ecuadorian Indigenous Confederation of the Highland
FEI	Ecuadorian Indigenous Federation
FOIN	Federation of Indigenous Peoples of Napo
FOISE	Indigenous Organizations of Sucumbíos, Ecuador
FUT	United Workers Union of Ecuador
IAF	Inter-American Foundation
IERAC	Ecuadorian Institute for Agrarian Reform and Colonization
IGO	International governmental organization
IITC	International Indian Treaty Council
ILO	International Labor Organization
IMF	International Monetary Fund
INGO	International non-governmental organization
IWGIA	International Working Group for Indigenous Peoples
MICH	Indigenous Movement of Chimborazo
MNC	Multinational Corporation
NCAI	National Congress of American Indians
NGO	Non-governmental organization
NRDC	National Resources Defense Council
NWF	National Wildlife Fund
OAS	Organization of American States
OISE	Organization of Secoya Indians
ONISE	Organization of Siona Indians
OPIP	Organization of Indigenous Peoples of Pastaza
Oxfam	Oxfam America - U.S.-based international NGO
Oxy	Occidental Oil Company
RAN	Rainforest Action Network
SAIIC	South American Indian Information Center
SLI	Summer Linguistic Institute
SMO	Social movement organization
TNC	Transnational Corporation

TSMO	Transnational social movement organization
WCIP	World Council of Indigenous Peoples
WRI	World Resources Institute
WWF	World Wildlife Fund

THE GLOBALIZATION OF
CONTENTIOUS POLITICS

CHAPTER ONE

Transcending Borders, an Introduction

I N JULY 1998, I RECEIVED A PHONE CALL FROM A SHUAR INDIAN NAMED
Kar, who was a former student and activist in the Amazonian indige-
nous rights movement of Ecuador. He was calling from a convenience
store in New York to let me know that he had arrived to the United
States to work and to help organize international resources for the Shuar
Indians in the Ecuadorian Amazon. During this conversation, he informed
me that a demonstration in front of a seismic testing site of ARCO Oil
Company was being planned by Quichua leaders, and friends of his in New
York, who were communicating with members of their organizations in
Puyo, Ecuador. Two days later, on the Internet in *El Hoy*, one of the
Ecuadorian national newspapers, I read about the demonstration of OPIP
in front of a seismic testing area of ARCO. This scenario of transnational
communication and network nodes is common and frequent among participants in the Amazonian indigenous rights movement.

This research project will illustrate the complex web of networks
and movements among Amazonian indigenous representatives, international non-governmental organization (INGO) representatives, multinational oil companies, and international funding agencies that has been
developing over the past fifteen or more years. Even though there are ethnic groups of Indians that still have not been contacted by Western individuals, such as Ecuador's Tagaeri, and the majority of Amazonian Indians
do not even travel to their capital cities, they have organized a system of
collective action outside of their state borders that has given a voice to
these once almost invisible groups. The reasons why this occurred, its
processes, and its outcomes will be analyzed in this project.

3

While the case of the Amazon and indigenous peoples relates a story that is not uncommon in the literature on collective action and ethnic conflict, it is distinct. Previously studied cases of collective action usually focus on resource-poor actors who organize and develop mobilization strategies against a target actor in their home country with the goal of obtaining policy change and other demands. Charles Tilly (1978) relates the story of strikes in 18th century England and France; Sidney Tarrow (1994) describes movement cycles in the United States, Western Europe, and Eastern Europe; and Doug McAdam tells the tale of civil rights activists in the 1960s. Their stories all have the common theme mentioned above and they take place within nation-states, seeking policy change and other outcomes within them.

However, the Amazonian story is distinct. These groups have formed networks and organizations outside of their localities; they have gained resources from international organization and multinational corporation (MNC) sources; and their strategies include a diverse array of transnational tactics from international boycotts to direct negotiations with multinational corporations. The environment of collective action has changed since the 18th century so that international market actors and other private, non-state actors have more influence in the international system and the political opportunity structure has broadened to include international actors.

Most of what we know about social movements is based in the nation-state and the domestic political system. However, social movements are not necessarily constrained by the state and in fact, mobilize across borders with other non-state actors. Recent examples of the transnationalization of social movements have been human rights, environmental, women's, and indigenous peoples movements.[1] Each of these movements utilizes resources from transnational actors, draws upon support from transnational organizations (intergovernmental and non-governmental), and acts to change policies and/or enter the political process of both the state and transnational organizations (such as the United Nations and the Organization of American States).

In addition to the increase of scholarship on the transnationalization of social movements, theories of globalization, global civil society, and the decline of the state have been articulated by scholars.[2] While states have not ceased to exist and the international system still functions via state institutions, leaders, and law, much of the social movement literature does not account for the dynamics of a global system in which multiple levels of political opportunities, resources, mobilizing structures, and policy outcomes exist[3].

This is not a new phenomenon in the international system. A world economy has existed for centuries and communication and diffusion of ideas among and between cultures and peoples has been well documented. However, the recent increase (since the 1960s) in non-state actors, coupled with the rapidity of communication and international travel,[4] have directly impacted not only state to state, or international institution to state relations, but they have directly altered the form of social movements (on a subnational level), imparting upon them a transnational frame and structure. Likewise, social movement organizations (SMOs) have transcended their national setting and have enmeshed their identities and ideas within the global arena. As Gary Marks and Doug McAdam note, "And, if indeed, institutionalized power is shifting away from the nation-state, then we would do well to relax the conceptual boundaries between these historically circumscribed political forms" (1995:97).

This project seeks to re-shape these "conceptual boundaries" in such a way that scholars of domestic politics and scholars of international politics can see reflections in the political activities of actors above and below the level of the state, and their interactions. I assume that the international system is not solely a dichotomy of anarchy and state sovereignty, but rather a plethora of actors with varying levels of authority, which includes, but is not exclusive to, states[5]. The assumption of authority of non-state actors in the international system (including actors of the societal level) provides the basis to analyze impacts and outcomes of transnational contentious politics on various levels from societal to international. This chapter will provide the roadmap for the rest of the project, outlining the assumptions and basis of the theory and the hypotheses.

CONTENTIOUS COLLECTIVE ACTION

Contentious political activity includes occasions when a collective, public, and aggrieved group of people challenges state/elite institutions through means which are not routinely utilized by state actors. Under this definition, contentious political activity includes rebellions, civil wars, ethnic conflict, social movements, and strikes.[6] This project focuses on the contentious political activity of social movements in an international context. Social movements may be defined as the sustained collective activity of an aggrieved group that shares common ends and joint activities to challenge power holders.[7] By focusing on the international sphere, collective action is no longer limited to state boundaries and outcomes are no longer limited to national outcomes. Thus, transnational contentious collective action is the globalization of local and national collective action in which domestic actors and international/transnational actors pursue common ends through joint activities. The type of collective action which will be analyzed in Ecuador through the indigenous movement is *transnational* contentious collective action because the collective activities executed by transnational and indigenous actors have been outside of the realm of state activities and have challenged state/elite and international authorities, institutions, and policies.

MNCS AS ACTORS IN TRANSNATIONAL CONTENTIOUS COLLECTIVE ACTION

Traditionally, the transnational relations and global civil society literatures have studied the impacts of international NGOs and IGOs on state policy outcomes (Lipschutz 1992; Raustiala nd). This framework expands the definition of transnational actors to include MNCs in the analysis. While I do agree that the primary motivation of firms is profit, they also act out of other motivations, such as social and environmental concerns.

The direct interaction and communication between multinational oil companies and indigenous peoples challenges the traditional economic, private nature of multinational enterprises (MNCs) and suggests a quasi-public role for MNCs in the global system. Furthermore, the inclusionary behavior of some oil MNCs with indigenous peoples demonstrates a change in MNC behavior from that of a private, autonomous actor, uninvolved in local/societal affairs, to that of a quasi-public actor which has direct impacts upon the mobilization and collective action strategies, and ultimately policy outcomes, of indigenous peoples. This project shows that some MNCs can be quasi-public actors that function on multiple levels within the international system, including subnational, national, and transnational.[8]

In order to analyze these transnational processes, MNCs must be examined as dynamic actors that have networks of communication and interaction with other transnational actors, such as international non-governmental organizations (INGOs) and inter-governmental organizations (IGOs); national actors, such as governmental leaders; and subnational/societal actors, including social movement organizations (SMOs) and national non-governmental organizations (NGOs). With respect to this project, oil MNCs in the Amazon have direct contact and negotiations with indigenous confederations (as will be demonstrated later), national NGOs, international NGOs, and state actors. They are an integral part of the transnational network of communication, mobilization, and policy outcomes. An analysis of transnational networks and transnational movements in Ecuador, or for that matter within a state with societies affected by MNCs, cannot overlook the significance of these actors.

THE CHANGING ROLE OF THE STATE IN THE
INTERNATIONAL SYSTEM

International relations literature recognizes the authority of actors via the dichotomy of state sovereignty and the anarchic international system. Since states are assumed to be sovereign and control outcomes within their borders, authority has been examined solely in relation to the state or state-to-state interactions (Cutler, Haufler, Porter 1996:11). However, this state-centric notion of authority neglects the analysis of non-state actors and the authority that they may possess in the international system. Authority will be analyzed as command over outcomes and the ability to make, decide, and enforce rules (Strange 1996:3; Viotti and Kauppi 1993:574). The recent mobilization of transnational actors and successful policy changes in response to issues such as human rights, the environment, women's rights, and indigenous rights suggests that non-state actors do possess a level of authority, or command over outcomes, within the international system. Moreover, the globalization of trade, finance, technology, and industry suggests that private, non-state actors at the international, national, and subnational levels possess an authority outside of the state system which warrants further analysis. As Susan Strange notes, "the authority in society and over economic transactions is legitimately exercised by agents other than states, and has come to be freely acknowledge by those who are subject to it" (Strange 1996: 13).

This project utilizes conceptions of public and private in order to analyze the international system. Notions of public and private permit non-state actors to be significant, influential elements of the international system, while still recognizing the international system of states and their sovereign authority. As Cutler cogently argues, liberalism establishes a dichotomy of space between public and private, such that public concerns the political, and private concerns the economic (1995:377). Public legitimate authority is "wielded by officials of the government who have gained that power to influence or command through any number of political means, most notable via elections" (Cutler, Haufler, Porter 1996:8). Private authority is perceived as neutral or apolitical, having to do with the natural economic cycle (Cutler 1995). The *problematique* which is analyzed throughout this project is the ability of private actors to obtain and maintain authority with respect to both political and economic spheres of activity on national and international levels. It also addresses the difficulty in distinguishing between public and private authority regarding oil MNCs, NGOs, INGOs, and indigenous confederations in Ecuador.

This project integrates the literatures of transnational relations, regime theory, global civil society, and collective action to form a model of transnational contentious collective action. The international system in which this model is based does not assume the primacy of state-power, but rather recognizes the existence of authority and influence from non-state actors on local/societal levels, national levels, and transnational levels. The authority of non-state actors not only influences structures and outcomes on an international level, but also on the level of social movements. Therefore, this idea of authority will be integrated into the literature of social movement theory, as well as international relations.

One of the fundamental assertions of social movement theory is that the modern social movement arose in response to the emergence of the modern nation-state (Tilly 1978). Social movement scholars have traditionally argued that state structures constrain or open political opportunities for social movement mobilization (Tilly 1978; Goldstone 1991; Tarrow 1994). The concept of political opportunity is enhanced in this study to include transnational actors who also provide political opportunities for group mobilization processes.

While most of the "new" research on transnational political opportunities has focused on the European Union,[9] this project demonstrates that political opportunities also exist via inter-governmental organizations, such as the United Nations, the Organization of American States, and the World Bank. With regard to the indigenous movement in Ecuador, when these inter-governmental organizations alter their structures or funding policies, transnational social networks and transnational social movements react in response to these changes. Moreover, transnational actors, such as MNCs, have the ability to change or influence political opportunity structures within the state. For example, in Ecuador, the high level of influence of multinational oil companies upon governmental structures and processes allows them to affect or change state institutions. Thus, the concept of political opportunity structures is broadened to include structures on international, national, and local levels.

CENTRAL THEMES

> This project seeks to advance research on transnational processes and their affects on the societal level by analyzing the following questions:

- Why and when does transnational contentious collective action emerge?
- What are the impacts of transnational contentious collective action?
- What are the different types of transnational contentious politics and how do we differentiate among them?

This research project augments our understanding in the literature of the transnational collective action process. This model outlines a process in which domestic political strategies become linked with international political opportunity structures. Moreover, MNCs are a part of this transnational network of actors and also play a role in domestic political strategy and outcomes.

The effects of transnational collective action are twofold: on one hand, domestic groups gain greater amounts of resources and influence due to their transnational mobilization strategies. However, these same strategies have deterred more coherent national movements from forming, and have increased competition among local actors for international funding sources. Former Minister of Education of Ecuador and participant in indigenous negotiations, Raúl Vallejo (1996), notes the deterioration of the national indigenous movement since the 1980s, when the transnational phase of collective action strategies began. Moreover, Alberto Taxzo, one of the Ecuadorian indigenous leaders in the 1990 national protest, stated that:

> As I have already explained, not only are there political parties in the country, or political institutions, there are also international institutions that sponsor them [indigenous organizations], as happened in the Continental Meeting of Indigenous Peoples, in which they [indigenous leaders] took thousands of dollars for their own pockets. Thus, of course there is a great tie, not only to the national part, but also to the international part...[translation by author] (Ramos 1990).

Thus, those who claim the globalization of civil society in which actors unite on a transnational level may be overlooking the fragmentation of the bases of societies due to the transnationalization of collective action strategies.

The case of Amazonian transnational collective action may be transplanted and tested upon other cases of resource-poor actors involved in issue areas which lend themselves to a transnational discourse, such as human rights, the environment, or women's rights. For example, in Nigeria, the Ogoni tribe is taking action in response to Shell Oil Company's extraction policies in their lands. In 1995, the Ogoni peoples, through INGO networks, contacted indigenous leaders from Ecuador to learn from their transnational strategies. Based on the findings from this project, actors are more likely to be successful when the issue area is highly contested or controversial internationally. In these cases, states are more likely to allow international actors to influence outcomes.

ORGANIZATION OF THE PROJECT

This project is divided into six chapters in total. The chapters that follow are empirical studies of the development, processes, and outcomes of the transnational collective action process. Chapter 2 emphasizes that theoretical underpinnings of the research and outlines the framework and model. My hypotheses, indicators, and overall research design are also detailed in this chapter. Chapter 3 illustrates the development of the transnational collective action process in the Amazon through a history of its international organizations and a detailed account of its networks in Ecuador. This chapter emphasizes the significance of historical factors in the collective action process and the change, over time, in international political opportunity structures. Finally, it details the domestic blockages in Ecuador that led to the adoption of transnational mobilization strategies.

Chapters 4 and 5 are the empirical case study chapters. Chapter 4 outlines the case of the Ecuadorian Amazonian transnational advocacy networks, their strategies, and the outcomes of their activities. This chapter highlights their interaction with multinational oil companies and the change in the behavior of oil companies in response to indigenous transnational mobilization tactics. Chapter 4 elucidates the intricacies of transnational advocacy networks and sets the stage for comparison with transnational social movement organizations (TSMO) in Chapter 5. Chapter 5 analyzes two TSMOs in the Amazon and the effectiveness of their mobilization strategies. It illustrates the developments of this high level of transnational collective action as well as the effects of such action.

Finally, Chapter 6 concludes the analysis by integrating the empirical evidence with the theoretical framework outlined in Chapter 2. In these conclusions, I turn to the question of effectiveness of transnational collective action and its travails. I end with a discussion of stronger and weaker theories of globalization and global civil society and analyze these theories in light of what I have learned from the empirical evidence presented in this study

NOTES

[1]For references to each of these social movements and their transnational links, see Alison Brysk (1994 and 1995); Margaret Keck and Katherine Sikkink (1995); Ro'nnie D. Lipschutz (1992); Thomas Princen and Matthias Finger, eds. (1994); Kathryn Sikkink (1993); and Paul Wapner (1995).[2] For example, see James Rosenau (1992); Paul Wapner (1996) James Riker (1995 and 1996); Philip Cerny (1995); M.J. Peterson (1992); and Ronnie D. Lipschutz (1992).

[3] Mobilizing structures are "those collective vehicles, informal as well as formal,

through which people mobilize and engage in collective action" (McAdam, McCarthy, and Zald 1996:3). As opposed to the grievance-based literatures of social movements, mobilization processes literatures focus on the organizational components of a movement and the organizational environment. The mobilization process drawn upon in this study is the combination of resource mobilization (McCarthy and Zald 1973, 1977) and political processes literatures (Tilly 1978), which emphasize not only formal group organization, but also informal, grassroots structures.

[4] A point noted by Sidney Tarrow (1994 and 1996); Jackie Smith (1994); and Thomas Risse-Kappen (1995).

[5] Authority will be defined as command over outcomes. The traditional realist approach to authority (i.e., Thucydides, Kenneth Waltz, Joseph Grieco)assumes that states are the sole and legitimate exercisers of authority in the international system. While liberal institutionalists (i.e., Robert Keohane) do acknowledge the existence of other transnational actors in the international system, they do not credit them with exercising command over outcomes in the international system. This idea of authority differs from the previous two ideas in that non-state, transnational actors may obtain authority and therefore, command influence over outcomes.

[6] Tilly, Charles (February 1996). "Contentious Politics and Social Change." New School for Social Research and Stockholm University.[7]McAdam, Doug, Sidney Tarrow, and Charles Tilly (1996): "To Map Contentious Politics," *Mobilization*: 1996.

[8]The term "national" refers to the domestic level of politics above the level of provinces, regions, or localities. It will be utilized in this manner throughout the project.

[9] See Marks, Gary and Doug McAdam "Social Movements and the Changing Structure of Political Opportunity in the European Union," in Imig, Doug and Sidney Tarrow (1995). "The Europeanization of Movements? Contentious Politics and the European Union, October 1983–March 1995." Paper presented at the ECSA Annual Conference at Charleston, S.C.

CHAPTER TWO

A Transnational Framework

HOW DO HISTORICALLY RESOURCE-POOR ACTORS CIRCUMVENT THE state level in order to gain policy outcomes and changes on domestic and transnational levels? This chapter will address the theoretical underpinnings of this question and of the broader project model. It combines the literatures of contentious politics, globalization, transnational relations, ethnic conflict, and multinational corporations to analyze the diverse and complex processes of transnational advocacy networks and transnational social movement organizations, in which the actors involved are ethnic groups, non-governmental organizations, international non-governmental organizations, the state, multi-lateral funding agencies, and multinational corporations. This chapter also maps out the hypotheses of the project and explains the methodology and research design.

FRAMEWORK FOR ANALYSIS

Transnational actors interact directly with sub-state, societal actors with increasing frequency in the international system. This direct link between the international sphere and the societal sphere challenges international relations scholars to search beyond the state as the primary unit of analysis. This research project assumes that the international system contains multiple levels of analysis, including transnational actors, the state, and societal actors.

One approach to analyzing the connection between the domestic political system and the international system is through a two-level game approach, which recognizes the constraints placed on national, elite actors in the international bargaining arena. Robert Putnam demonstrates the constraints of national leaders in the international sphere who are bound to their domestic allies, and seek international bargains that satisfy their domestic coalitions (1988: 434). Moreover, actors may have varying loyalties when operating at different levels, depending upon the optimal choice available for the actor in that arena, such that domestic leaders may concede sovereignty to international organizations in some issue areas (Tsebelis 1990). The two-level approach to international relations, recognizing direct influences of the international and domestic systems on one another, provides a useful framework for understanding the various influences and constraints placed upon actors in the international system.

However, the two-level approach stops short of analyzing actors below the state level who may not be included in the official policy process of the state, such as social movements. A multiple level approach to the international system acknowledges the presence of actors within society who supersede the formal state policy process and utilize transnational actors to influence domestic policy on their behalf. In the case of the indigenous people's movement in Latin America, indigenous organizations have created links with transnational actors to influence national and international policy. Through these transnational links, indigenous peoples have gained greater access to national and international policy processes, while also circulating information about their agenda in the international sphere.

This study also builds upon the Gurr and Harff model by identifying transnational actors who coordinate with ethnic groups, and their impacts upon group mobilization, protest, and rebellion. Ted Robert Gurr and Barbara Harff (1994) examine the role of the international system on "ethnopolitical conflict" through their consideration of external support to a group and the status of the regime. They assume that certain elements of the international system and domestic policymaking processes affect one another. Moreover, this study examines ethnic groups as pro-active members within the international system, such that ethnic groups are part of a transnational contentious collective action process[1], rather than solely reactive to the international and domestic systems[2].

The Gurr and Harff model is applicable to my study in that it links the international and domestic systems by focusing on the role of external support in mobilization. Moreover, their focus on "ethnic" conflict highlights the significance of ethnic identity in a movement. My study examines how transnational actors impact the movement, including the factors that contribute to the mobilization processes, such as identity. Thus, I employ frameworks from social movement and ethnic conflict theories.

While not directly addressing the social movement literature, Franke

Wilmer utilizes a "world system approach," asserting the internationalization of the indigenous movement, yet not solely based on evidence from the Latin American experience. Wilmer notes that the arbitrary borders of states in the present international system are based upon boundaries devised by modern European nation-states. The sovereignty of these states is protected through an international and regional system of institutions. However, indigenous communities were not constructed within these implanted state boundaries (14–16). These indigenous communities currently present a challenge to traditional state borders and claims to sovereignty.

Although indigenous groups were marginalized for many years, Wilmer argues that they have greatly expanded their efforts to protect their traditions, culture, and resources. NGOs held preliminary global hearings on indigenous rights in 1971 and 1974, and in 1975, the World Council of Indigenous Peoples was founded, receiving consultative status in the United Nations. By 1977, the Indigenous Peoples' Network (IPN) was founded, with the purpose of developing a world-view of the indigenous movement. Moreover, the United Nations has incorporated a Working Group on Indigenous Populations (as of 1982), which is currently considering a draft declaration for the international protection of indigenous peoples' rights (Wilmer 1993:18–20). This transnational contentious collective action was prompted not only by organization from below (such as societies), but also by changes in the political opportunity structures of international intergovernmental organizations. Thus, the state is no longer the only focus of action for the indigenous groups of Latin America and elsewhere.

Wilmer contends that international politics does not sufficiently address collective action because it assumes that the state is the primary actor in the international system. She argues for a re-conceptualization of the international system in which the unit of analysis goes beyond the state to the societal community, thus considering indigenous peoples as "political actors" within the system. The state is legitimated through its support from society, and thus, in a global context, societies must be analyzed as a separate basis of power and influence. Wilmer describes the relationship between the state and the societal community as "symbiotic." According to Wilmer, the international system may be viewed as:

> an image of intersecting political communities,... by which the basis of state power derives from the context of the political community of states, which is subject to change as a result of changes taking place within the state and in interstate relations (1993:44).

This project shares Wilmer's conceptualization of the international system.

I view the international system as a multi-level process with varying authoritative actors from the societal level to the state and transnational level.

From her world system perspective, Wilmer cites four elements in the emerging world system. First, "international interaction has expanded from a basically Eurocentric to a global proportion." Second, there is an increase in communication and technology. Third, this "communication has made possible the emergence of shared norms derived from those who led the expansionary movement." Fourth, "patterns of interaction and discourse in international relations today can best be understood by defining the context as a 'society'" (1993:171–172). From this perspective, Wilmer asserts that a global civil society may be evolving, and the indigenous peoples' movement is an example of the emergence of norms in the international system that challenges the traditional sovereignty of the state. The Amazonian indigenous movement exemplifies this challenge to state sovereignty through its transnational organization.

Scholars of transnational relations also assert that the international system and domestic systems interact. Transnational relations literature evolved in the early 1970s and focused on "the movement of items (tangible or intangible) across state boundaries when at least one actor is not an agent of a government or an intergovernmental organization" (Nye and Keohane 1971:332). Effects of these relations were: 1) attitude changes, 2) international pluralism, 3) increases in constraints on states through dependence and interdependence, 4) increases on the ability of certain governments to influence others, and 5) the emergence of autonomous actors with private foreign policies. The purpose of these early studies was to determine the impacts of transnational actors on states and the international system.

Transnational relations studies were supplanted by regime theory studies in the late 1970s and early 1980s[3]. However, recently a new wave of transnational relations studies has emerged. Thomas Risse-Kappen defines transnational relations as:

> regular interactions across national boundaries when at least one actor is a non-state agent or does not operate on behalf of a national government or an intergovernmental organization (1995:3).

The emergent literature on transnational relations does not solely examine the impacts of non-state actors on state policies, but it also examines the impacts of these actors upon societal forces. Moreover, it differs from regime theory by emphasizing the reliance of transnational actors on information to form networks among one another.[4] Transnational networks help "to define the issue area itself, convince target audiences that the problems thus defined are soluble, prescribe solutions, and monitor their implementation" (Keck and Sikkink 1998: 5).

M.J. Peterson remarks that any conception of international society must take into account:

> the transnational activities of individuals, firms, interest associations and societal groups. These societal actors have significant effects on the flow of material resources, know-how and ideas around the world, and cannot be ignored in any full account of international relations. (1992: 371).

Transnational links between countries have not only affected the state's institutions and elites, but sub-state social movements as well. Previous scholarship that assumed MNCs were targets of collective action and protest must be re-examined. Peterson argues that MNC policies and motives are varied and may have different transnational impacts upon societies, states, and the international system. MNCs vary greatly in type, organization, motives, and structure, and cannot be categorized into one type of instrumental, economic actor[5]. This project will examine the complex motivations of MNCs as part of an "international society" and the change in their behavior since the oil boom in Ecuador in the early 1970s, and its impacts on indigenous peoples and policy outcomes in Ecuador.

Lines between MNCs and NGOs are no longer so clear, as regime theorists had once speculated. As Virginia Haufler demonstrates, private regimes "institutionalize agreements among non-state actors and regularly negotiate their conflicts" (1993:13). Haufler describes private actors as firms and private voluntary organizations (PVOs), such as the International Planned Parenthood Federation, both of which have played key roles in transnational policy coalitions that influenced national policies, but through different resources. PVOs are unlikely to form regimes, but rather operate through domestic coalitions and information exchange. Firms, on the other hand, may "operate through the domestic political system to influence inter-state regimes" (1993:10).

Haufler observes that corporate private regimes cooperate beyond price and market share. Rather, these firms "institutionalize agreements among non-state actors and regularly negotiate their conflicts" (Haufler 1993:13). Furthermore, she remarks that NGOs are not always without private motivations and that information exchange and transfer of norms takes place between social forces and firms, in addition to the traditionally studied exchange between NGOs and societal forces. The conceptualization of non-governmental organizations as PVOs facilitates characterization of NGOs as "purposive" rather than "principled" actors. By categorizing international non-governmental organizations as "principled," we lack an understanding of the diverse interests and goals of these groups.[6]

Haufler notes the embeddedness of firms in global civic culture. She asserts that in business areas which "... social groups perceive a strong ethical or moral content," such as "... conservation of biological diversity," firms operate within a larger cultural context (1996:12). Stopford and Strange refer to the embeddedness of a firm in the societal culture as the "good citizen" (1991:225). For instance, firms have changed their policies to incorporate ecological safety measures. Ecuadorian MNCs have changed their behavior, through learning and key individual communications over time, to include indigenous peoples in their policymaking processes and to clean areas of the rainforest and its rivers contaminated by petroleum. The role of MNCs has expanded to include negotiation, not only on business policies, but also environmental plans, social plans, and in some cases, talks of profit- sharing between MNCs and indigenous organizations have emerged. Thus, MNCs have developed over time strategies of negotiation with key players rather than strictly profit-oriented bargaining. MNCs have also provided resources for indigenous organizations. Direct negotiations with MNCs have not only affected the Amazonian indigenous social movements and their mobilizing structures, but have also challenged our perceptions of the functions of MNCs in the global system. The networks and alliances between MNCs, other non-state transnational actors, and societal-level social movements will be further explored in the project.

However, MNCs are not the only actors involved in transnational contentious collective action. Non- corporate actors, such as INGOs, are part of the transnational exchange of information aimed at national and international policy change. When private actors such as MNCs, NGOs, social movement organizations (SMOs), and INGOs collectively organize and mobilize, it is more likely that the result will be networks and alliances based upon common goals and interests. When these networks and alliances form based on an issue area, such as human rights or the environment, private actors may take on quasi-public roles in order to implement policy change. Thus, the activation of transnational networks may politicize a private actor and convert a once private authority to a position of public actor. The case of oil MNCs in Ecuador illustrates this situation in which private actors, oil MNCs, have formed networks with PVOs and SMOs, thus changing their behavior toward indigenous peoples as well as their nature to a quasi-public authority.

The penetration of the MNC in all levels of the international system from local to transnational has spawned the term "glocalization" (Sanchez-

Parga 1997: 32). José Sanchez-Parga argues that the MNC is so powerful in the international system that it not only influences state policies and structures, but also local level structures and organizations. He further notes that interaction, such as networks, with MNCs has fostered a change in societal organization, political culture, and governability on a regional and local level (1997:33). Oil MNCs in the Ecuadorian Amazon and the transnational networks and movements formed around this region have "glocalized" its impacts, such that outcomes of the transnational contentious collective action are observed on multiple levels and with varying effects.

The term "global civil society" has also captured the essence of "glocalization," focusing on the authority of transnational actors and their ability create a civil society on a global level. Ronnie D. Lipshutz examines the rise of a global civil society in which transnational political networks emerge among domestic and international actors, challenging the nation-state system from above and below. The indigenous rights movement is an example of such *glocalizing* processes in that local indigenous groups have established networks with other indigenous groups outside of their state boundaries and other transnational actors in order to pursue goals of legal recognition of their ethnic groups and environmental control over the lands on which they live.

Paul Wapner also analyzes the growing trend in transnational contentious collective action through the role of non-governmental organizations (NGOs) in international environmental activism. He posits that there is a civil society, or "associational life," which exists "below the state and across national boundaries" (Wapner 1995: 313).[7] In Wapner's view of world politics, the state system is significant, but does not address transnational activism that has occurred in recent history (Wapner 1996).

The framework for this project thus intersects with three bodies of literature: ethnic conflict, transnational relations, and social movement theory. It considers the significance of ethnic identity in group mobilization, as well as the impacts of domestic discriminatory policies. This is derived from the ethnic conflict literature. The emphasis on group mobilization and policy outcomes is drawn from social movement theory. Finally, transnational relations models provide links between society, the state, and the international system. These three bodies of literature provide the architecture for a more comprehensive analysis of the process and outcomes of transnational contentious collective action.

Hypothesis #1

Given the evidence of linkages between transnational actors and societal actors, I propose that *(H1) transnational contentious collective action emerges a) when there are constraints and blockages in the domestic system; b) when there are international political opportunities and mobilizing structures which create openings for resource-poor actors; and c) when the interests of domestic groups and transnational actors complement each other.* Impermeability of state structures/institutions constrains or blocks domestic movements, particularly resource-poor groups, preventing them from mobilizing for policy outcomes or changes. *State constraints and blockages* will be identified as a lack of representation of indigenous peoples within state institutions, such as the National Congress, Ministries, and the Executive Branch.

The concept of *state impermeability* derives from the transnational relations scholarship of Margaret Keck and Kathryn Sikkink. Keck and Sikkink demonstrate, through their analysis of female foot binding in China, that transnational advocacy networks are more likely to emerge when "the channels between domestic groups and their governments are severed or hampered" (1998: 3). They equate transnational issues with the "master frames" of the social movement literature in which movements frame an issue around the larger belief system which they would like to affect.[8]

Craig Jenkins and Kurt Schock argue, "A healthy corrective, then, is to look at recent thinking about global structures and their impact on states and domestic conflicts, especially as they bear on Third World states" (Jenkins and Schock 1992: 175). These authors assert that international factors such as economic policies, transnational investments, and military intervention have greatly impacted groups within the states of the Third World.

Taking a more structural approach, Jack Goldstone analyzes collective action and conflict through three elements: 1) state resources; 2) "elite disunity and alienation from the state;" and 3) "a high level of mass mobilization potential" (Goldstone, Gurr, and Moshiri 1991:30–31). The first element of Goldstone's model addresses this hypothesis: state resources. Building on his approach, I propose that transnational action emerges when state resources are not provided to the social movement, thus prompting them to look to the international level for aid.

The state is a significant variable in this model, not only due to its domestic resources, but also because of its transnational nature. The sovereignty of the state in the international system is continually challenged, particularly by transnational non-state actors (i.e., NGOs). As illustrated in the research on transnational ecological movements, states feel pressures "through multiple channels, including intergovernmental relations, dealing with international organizations, transnational linkages among environmental groups, and the workings of the media" (Conca 1994:701). The state is not a static factor, but one that is dynamic and changes in response to the global system. Thus, state resources must be approached not only on a domestic level, but also accounting for the transnational character of the state. Although the state is not always the authoritative actor in the international system, the global system was founded upon a system of states which still influences interactions within the global arena. As discussed earlier, all states are subject to penetration by the global economy and transnational actors.

This framework suggests that weak states, which are dependent upon the resources of a firm, are more penetrable to private authority and actors than are strong states which do not depend upon the resources of a firm. As Stopford and Strange (1991) posit, governments are faced with new challenges due to changing world structures. Moreover, multinationals are not "monolithic" actors and managers are increasingly becoming statesmen. Thus, the role of states is significant, but they are actors in the global arena bargaining for authority over other transnational, private actors.

States have a close interaction with private actors, societal and transnational. Peter Evans (1995) argues that firms and states have shared economic interests. Economic transformation is most likely to occur when states have achieved a level of "embedded autonomy," in which the state and private actors are connected, yet the state is insulated from domination by private actors. Eduardo Silva (1996) asserts that these dense networks of communication between firms and government leaders are crucial for influencing the private sector's confidence to commit resources for development programs. While both of these conceptions are useful, they do not account for a state, which does not represent the majority of its societal forces, such that alliances with firms only facilitate economic success, but not social representation and equity. In cases where the state is struggling to maintain legitimacy over a population in which some elements may be challenging it, alliances with firms and not social forces could increase the possibility of contention and violence against the state being challenged by private actors from below and from above. Rather than conceiving of the state as an authoritative, sovereign actor or a partner with economic, private actors, I view the state as a multi-faceted body consisting of multiple institutions. The state seeks to interact with private actors from both transnational and sub-national levels. At times, it is in the interest of a state to remain out of negotiations between transnational actors and societal actors, such as cases in which the state can place blame on private actors or the state does not have the resources to be involved (i.e., technological, knowledge-information, etc.). At times when state sovereignty is challenged, or the legitimacy of the regime is challenged, the state has greater incentive to be involved in actions and negotiations between transnational and sub-national actors. As Roger Normand, policy director of the Center for Economic and Social Rights, commented on the relation among oil MNCs, the state, and indigenous peoples, "Ecuador's indigenous and environmental organizations have pushed human rights groups to re-examine their exclusive focus on government actors" (Jochnik 1995:8). Furthermore, an attorney for the Sierra Club Legal Defense Fund commented that government institutions are so under-funded and understaffed that most monitoring responsibilities remain in the "hands of the corporations themselves" (Jochnik 1995:8). Thus, states may abdicate their responsibilities and authority to private actors under certain conditions.

This also implies that states are facilitating the private authority of actors. Thus, states are actors in a bargaining process in which firms, transnational organizations, and societal forces are a part. It may be the case, based on these observations, that in certain issue areas the state is precluded from having an authoritative role. These issue areas would be those of "strong moral or ethical content," similar to those which were previously asserted to influence a firm.[9] Therefore, states may have restraints on their authority on issues such as environmental protection, human rights, or ethnic conflict. These restraints allow other transnational actors (private and public) to influence state and sub-state policies and actions[10]. These restraints on state authority impact the political opportunity structures for a transnational social network or transnational social movement.

Political opportunity structure is defined as "the dimensions of the political environment that provide incentives for people to undertake collective action by affecting their expectation for success or failure" (Tarrow 1994: 85). Collective action scholars, such as Charles Tilly (1978) and Sidney Tarrow (1994), assert that group internal or external resources facilitate a group's political opportunity. Tilly identifies five variables in his "mobilization model:" 1) interest, 2) organization, 3) mobilization, 4) collective action, and 5) opportunity/threats. He argues that the main determinants of a group's mobilization are its organization, it interests, and its current opportunity or threats. The result of a group's power, mobilization, and opportunities is collective action. Tilly analyzes the collective action process and its intensity from mobilization through revolution. He argues that the analysis of the entire process in episodic "snapshots," permits researchers to understand the complex process leading to rebellion and revolution (1978:54–56,230).

More recently, Tarrow argues that social movements are crossing state boundaries, such as the conflict between France and Spain over fishing in the Canadian waters. Tarrow suggests that actors in this conflict were engaged at different levels, ranging from the local fishermen's organizations in Galicia to the European Union (EU). He cites the rapid increase in communication and travel as contributing to the increase in the impact of global factors on social movements (Tarrow 1995:12–16).

While traditional social movement literature only cites domestic institutions as creating political opportunities, new studies have provided evidence that transnational political opportunities do exist and are impacting a new wave of transnational social networks and movements (Tarrow 1996; Imig and Tarrow 1996; Marks and McAdam 1996). This project seeks to understand the impacts of expanding political opportunities in a globalizing world.

Alison Brysk (1994) also analyzes the opening of political opportunity structures by transnational actors. She utilizes the literatures of transnational relations and social movements to address the transnational organization of indigenous groups in Latin America. Brysk argues that indigenous groups mobilize on the national and international levels. She asserts that transnational movements mobilize from above (i.e., the international system) and from below (i.e.,the group). According to her model, the pressure from international actors and domestic, group actors influences the state, leading to an opening of opportunity for the group. International environmental and human rights NGOs and international organizations, such as the United Nations, have provided an international opening in which indigenous groups have mobilized. The indigenous movement of Ecuador provides a case in which indigenous peoples have made links with MNCs, NGOs, IGOs, and foreign governments (Treakle 1998). Therefore, this study will combine the work of Haufler and Peterson regarding MNCs, and the work of Keck, Sikkink, Brysk, et. al. regarding NGOs, to understand how both types of transnational actors affect the social movement process of indigenous peoples.

Based on these studies, this framework expands the concept of political opportunity to the international level, or *transnational political opportunities*. The concept of transnational political opportunities is identified through resources provided by transnational actors for social movements. These actors are not confined to one state, but rather act across state boundaries through multiple levels, such as international, state, and sub-state/societal levels. The transnational resources that provide political opportunities for societal actors include:

1 communication and market access and information

2 material resources

3 non-monetary resources

4 diplomatic and ideological support (See Gurr 1994: Revised Minorities at Risk Code Sheet).[11]

The higher the level of transnational resources, the more likely the emergence of transnational contentious collective action.

These elements affect the emergence of transnational contentious collective action because they provide resources for societal actors that were not provided by the state. Moreover, societal actors may be empowered by these resources, which may open political opportunities for them to challenge state or transnational actor policies.

In summary, hypothesis #1 addresses the globalization of social movements by examining the expansion of political opportunity and resources for social movements beyond the domestic sphere to transnational actors. In doing so, it synthesizes domestic frameworks for analyzing political opportunity, represented by Charles Tilly among others, with frameworks of transnational networks, such as those by Alison Brysk and Kathryn Sikkink and Margaret Keck. Thus, it tests the influence of transnational actors on domestic structures and society, and society's impact upon transnational actors.

Hypothesis #2

Collective action is joint activity in pursuit of common ends. These common ends may be identified through the objectives that group leaders articulate and pursue. I assume that the goals of the indigenous movement in Ecuador are policy change, either through formal outcomes, or access to the policy process through state or transnational structures. In order to determine what impacts transnational contentious collective action has on the a) group and b) policy process or outcomes, I will test the hypothesis that *(H2.A) transnational contentious collective action a) will lead to change in the collective action strategies of the domestic group on national and international levels; and will (H2.B) expand policy change and outcomes to a national level within the state and a transnational level within NGOs, IGOs, or MNCs.* As collective activity expands challenges to a national level, elites on the national level are more likely to respond positively. Therefore, transnational contentious collective action must be studied not only through its effects upon mobilization, but also its effects upon state and international policy outcomes, changes, and access to the process. The outcomes examined in this analysis are not the sole outcomes that may be expected from transnational contentious collective action. There is potential for long term outcomes of this form of collective action, such as impacts upon the national social movement, that will be expanded in future works.

Again drawing upon Goldstone's framework for analyzing collective action, I utilize his second concept, "elite disunity and alienation from the state" (Goldstone 1991:38). Transnational contentious collective action also influences elite loyalties to the state. As transnational actors provide resources to the domestic group, and collective action rises, the action expands from local and regional levels to a national level. As this occurs, elites on the national level are likely to respond to transnational contentious collective action demands. This response legitimates the societal group within the national political process.

Thomas Rochon and Daniel Mazmanian suggest that:

> Access to the policy process is the most effective path for movement organizations to have an impact on policy outcomes, because authorities are often more willing to offer inclusion in the process than they are to accept movement demands for policy change (1993: 75).

They analyze the changes in the policy process that involve the inclusion of new groups or means of dialogue between the government and the social movement organization. They also expand upon Gamson's dimension of success, policy change and inclusion, by adding a third factor, changing social values. They identify changing social values through a change in what is considered *political* within the national system and also through the appearance of the social movement's issues on the political agenda (1993:77).   This study will expand the notion of *successful collective action* to include the results of transnational contentious collective action. In order to determine its effects, I will examine not only direct policy outcomes and changes, but also the inclusion of indigenous issues in the political agenda of the Executive branch and the National Congress. This can be identified through elections, campaigns, and party platforms. According to my proposition, transnational contentious collective action will move the political agendas from regional to national significance due to the influence of transnational actors within the process. Thus, transnational actors create an opening within the policy process which was not previously present for indigenous groups.

Sidney Tarrow also recognizes the complex policy system in which collective action participants become involved when they insert themselves in policy networks. Although political opportunities create resources and openings for group mobilization, "cycles of protest" further create opportunities for elites within the government to respond to social movements. Cycles of protest respond to a complex cultural and political matrix of meanings, in which social movements and elites offer proposals and counter proposals with regard to the demands of the social movement organization. In this study, I propose that transnational actors increase the resources for domestic groups to counter elite proposals.

The outcomes of social movements have further complicated the process. Tarrow attributes changing cycles of protest to the rise in global communications. He argues that "If movements are becoming transnational, they may be freeing themselves of state structures, and thence of the constraining influence of state mediated contention" (1994: 196). Thus, hypothesis #2 not only focuses on the expansion of policy changes and outcomes on a national level, but also an international level, such that transnational actors may also change their policies toward indigenous peoples.

The concept of *strategy change* will be identified through new forms of mobilization. Indicators for strategy change include:

1. The degree of use of transnational actor resources, such as newsletters, or ideological or diplomatic support
2. The degree of use of global media and communications technology
3. The degree of travel to other regions or countries to increase support for their organization.

The concept of *expansion of collective activity to a national level* implies that the activity of the group has increased from local or regional protests to national protests. Indicators for this expansion to the national level include:

1. The number of protests of the domestic group outside of the locality or region
2. The extent to which, and ways in which, other national actors are involved in the group activity
3. The extent to which, and ways in which, the state, or national policy is identified as the target of the mobilization

The concept of expansion of collective activity to an international level is defined as the contentious collective activity of a social movement across state boundaries in conjunction with other non-state actors. Indicators for this expansion to the international level include:

1. The number of protests of the domestic group outside of the state
2. The extent to which, and ways in which, other non-state

actors are involved in the group activity
3. The extent to which, and ways in which, supranational organizations and policy is identified as the target of the mobilization

The concept of *expansion of policy change or outcome to the national level* will be identified as any policy change on a national level that affects indigenous peoples. Indicators for national level policy change include:

1. The number and type of National Congressional policies that comply with indigenous demands
2. The number and type of National Ministry policies that comply with indigenous demands
3. The extent to which, and way in which, national party platforms address indigenous demands
4. The extent to which, and way in which, indigenous actors are included in the state policy process[12]

The concept of *expansion of policy change or outcomes to the transnational level* will be identified as any policy change on an international level that affects indigenous peoples. Indicators for transnational level policy change include:

1. The number and type of international NGO policies that address indigenous demands
2. The number and type of MNC policies that address indigenous demands
3. The number and type of IGO policies that address indigenous demands
4. The extent to which, and way in which, indigenous actors are included in the policy processes of transnational actors[13]

The breakdown of authoritarian regimes and the development of democratic institutions in Latin America created political opportunities for new social movements. Arturo Escobar and Sonia E. Alvarez remark that new social movements in Latin America redefined collective identity within the state to include new communities (1992:4). Groups that were previously not recognized by the state, or were not previously mobilized, asserted themselves in the political system throughout the 1980s. The new social movement literature in Latin America illustrates the expansion of social movements from local levels to the national political arena.

Scholars of new social movements in Latin America, such as Escobar, Alvarez, Susan Eckstein, and Judith Adler Hellman, argue that collective identities and social networks are important factors to consider in this region's social movements. Hellman argues that these social movements have influenced the policy process and party system to include new groups on the political agenda and within the national political debate (1992:59). Both Escobar and Hellman assert that the scholarship on social movements based on European and North American models needs to be broadened to include the new phenomena in developing countries.

New social movements are also products of new structural developments of the state. For instance, Calderon, Piscitelli, and Reyna argue that new technologies and economic globalization have not only affected state institutions and leaders, but they have inspired the establishment of new movements. They cite the economic adjustment policies of states, influenced by the International Monetary Fund, as catalysts for political action of many poor communities (1992:31). Deborah Yashar attributes "political liberalization reforms" on the rural population as one factor that has stimulated renewed activism among indigenous peoples (1998:32). Rodolfo Stavenhagen (1984) and Héctor Díaz Polanco (1988) assert that the indigenous movement is not only affecting the role of the state from a societal level, but has also mobilized with international actors, such as the United Nations and activist NGOs, to influence policy change.

Due to this internationalization of social movements, Escobar and Alvarez remark that students of new social movements must produce a cross-cultural, transnational theory to explain the impacts of globalization upon societies and collective identities (1992:13). Susan Eckstein also contends that international forces are important factors influencing social movements, yet she highlights global economic interests in Latin America and national elite responses to these pressures as key factors[14]. As will be analyzed through the Ecuadorian case, global economic and non-economic forces have impacted the indigenous movement directly, and MNC behavior has changed since the 1970s. Thus, this study will examine the transnational effectiveness of social movements.

The literature on social movements in Ecuador attributes the emergence of collective action and community mobilization to the development of democratic institutions after the transition to democracy in 1979. While most scholars of Ecuador agree that informal, social networks had been established well before democratic transition, the political opening provided means for formal organization and protest. Throughout the 1980s, these new social movements re-defined "the political" within the state of Ecuador to include such new identities as women's movements and indigenous movements. This study attributes the rise of the indigenous movement not only to domestic political openings under democratization, but also to the resources provided by transnational actors.

Amy Conger Lind remarks that the women's movement of Ecuador principally emerged as a community-based movement. However, it developed into a national movement through expanded networks with other women's organizations throughout Latin America, including international organizations such as the United Nations and the Organization of American States. As social networks of women grew between regions and international actors, policy outcomes were focused on a national level, including the foundation of the National Office of Women in the mid-1980s.

Indigenous issues also framed political debate through an organized, national movement. Leon Zamosc (1994) examines the 1990 indigenous *levantamientos*, or uprisings,[15] in the Sierra region through a combination of structural factors and resource mobilization of the CONAIE. Zamosc argues that the highland indigenous groups, primarily Quichua, have a collective identity, formed through an historical process of community agrarian living. State structural changes, such as the Agrarian Reform Law, threatened the traditional indigenous interdependence with the communal land system. Although Zamosc identifies external factors of mobilization, such as development agencies and the Catholic Church, he does not analyze their impacts upon the indigenous movements in the Sierra.

Melina Selverston (1994) examines the relationship between the state and the indigenous peoples of Ecuador. She argues that indigenous organization and protest on a national level have created a national identity for indigenous peoples and have placed them within the national political debate and agenda. She points to indigenous representatives in national, provincial, and local bodies as signs of increasing awareness of the movement on a national level. Moreover, indigenous issues have been incorporated in political party agendas. However, Selverston does not identify the role of international factors within the indigenous social movement, including the significance of business interests within the policy process of Ecuador and the impacts that they have had on indigenous policy issues.

Carrie A. Meyer (1998) and Kay Treakle (1998) note the increase in international NGOs and multi-lateral development bank participation in the indigenous rights movement in Ecuador. However, both scholars fail to analyze the significance of MNCs in the process. Meyer focuses on NGOs and Treakle on the importance of funding from multi-lateral funding agencies. The studies in this project add MNCs as not just peripheral or target actors, but integral components of the transnational advocacy network in Ecuador.

In the case of Ecuador, Latin America's second largest oil producing country (following Venezuela), over fifty percent of the national income is earned through its largest export, petroleum, and thus, the economy is highly influenced by the multinational oil industry. For instance, in the late 1980s, the decline in international oil prices adversely affected Ecuador's debt repayment program. As Catherine Conaghan and John Malloy (1995) demonstrate, business interest groups throughout the 1980s played pivotal roles in influencing modernization policies of the state. In particular, multinational industry representatives and mining industry representatives were influential in campaign financing and support of economic policies from the Executive Branch of the government. (Martz 1987). The economic and political significance of petroleum is similar in other resource-rich Latin American countries. Thus, resource development of petroleum and minerals defines and constrains much of the political policies and processes in Ecuador, and other Latin American countries. Studies of transnational actors cannot overlook the significance of MNCs in the process. Ecuador provides a case in which indigenous peoples have mobilized on a transnational level for protest and change in national and international policy outcomes and processes.[16]

In summary, hypothesis #2 also utilizes social movement and collective action frameworks to understand how groups influence policy outcomes and what factors change group strategies. The indigenous movement of Ecuador provides an example of a case in which domestic and transnational factors influence policy outcomes and strategies of the movement. Hypothesis #2 expands the analysis to include transnational actors, thus contributing a new dimension to the study of social movements and their impact on the policy processes of domestic and transnational actors.

Hypothesis #3

This research project will analyze the impacts of transnational actors upon social movements and their collective action cycles. I assume that identity (including race, ethnicity, religion, and gender), networks, and framing are important factors in the emergence and sustenance of a social movement. While I concur that rational choice frameworks for analyzing social movements and collective action provide helpful tools for analysis, this study will also examine issues of the individual beyond self-interest, such as collective identity, grievances, common purpose, and ethnicity. Therefore, I combine aspects of resource-mobilization (RM), structural theories, and the literature on ethnic conflict.

Indigenous peoples of Ecuador organize nationally and coordinate national protests under the CONAIE. While they are organized throughout the country in smaller local and regional indigenous organizations, Sierra (highland peoples) form coalitions with Amazonian peoples and vice versa. Although each indigenous group differs by region and ethnicity, i.e., Quichua, Huaorani, Cofán, they identify on a broader scale as being indigenous.[17] Therefore, studies which analyze collective action solely as action based on individual utilitarian models provide an incomplete account of group mobilization based on shared community culture, social networks, and identity.[18]

Recent studies of transnational contentious collective action (Smith 1996; Tarrow 1995; Imig and Tarrow 1996; Marks and McAdam 1996) have acknowledged the existence of networks that expand outside state realms and the use of international discourses and ideas to create "master frames" in their process of mobilization. Two factors which existing social movement theory has held constant are identity and social networks. These two factors provide the basis for group organization and mobilization. However, transnational contentious collective action, in which actors are forming networks across state boundaries and losing their spatial closeness, raises questions about the nature of networks and identity in the process of globalization. Recent studies of these phenomena leave two questions relatively unexplored:

1. What is the significance of networks and identity when spatial relationships globalize?
2. Are all transnational collective activities transnational social movements, or are there differences in the degree of transnational contentious collective action?

Roger Gould (1995), in his work on Parisian insurgents in the 19th century and Doug McAdam (1988), in his research on <u>Freedom Summer</u> volunteers, argue that social ties are indispensable for creating collective identity. These social ties are created and maintained in environments of close social contact and exchange. If this is true, then how do transnational collective activities overcome these spatial boundaries?

I suggest that social networks and collective identities are increasingly likely to expand in a world where transportation and communication is rapid and inexpensive. Exchange of ideas and social connections may no longer need to be in the same room or community, but rather take place in the larger global community. Thus, the concept of spatial closeness may no longer be necessary in analyzing transnational contentious collective action.[19]

Based on the above assumptions, *(H3) I contend that the level of integration between domestic social movements and transnational actors impacts the degree of severity of transnational contentious collective action. Therefore, transnational advocacy networks lead to sustained, yet non-integrated, social networks with collective action centered on a particular issue-area. Transnational social movements lead to sustained and integrated social networks with transnationally and nationally-centered collective action strategies and goals.*

Sidney Tarrow (1996) has developed a useful topology for examining transnational contentious collective action, which differentiates "transnational interactions" on a scale from temporary and non-integrated interaction to sustained and integrated interaction in domestic social networks. Transnational diffusion is the least sustained and least integrated form of transnational interaction in which forms of collective action, symbols, and movements spread from one country to another. The second least sustained and least integrated form is transnational political exchange which "involves actors from different countries with ideological affinities, each of which has something to gain from the relationship and offers something to the other" (1996:22).

Transnational advocacy networks and transnational social movements are respectively the most sustained and most integrated forms of transnational contentious collective action, and will be the forms on which this project concentrates. Drawing upon the work of Margaret Keck and Kathryn Sikkink, transnational advocacy networks include:

> the set of relevant actors working internationally on an issue who are bound together by shared values, a common discourse, and dense exchanges of information and services. Such networks are most prevalent in issue areas characterized by high value content and informational uncertainty. They involve actors from non-governmental and intergovernmental organizations, and are increasingly present in such issue areas as human rights, women's rights, and the environment (Keck and Sikkink 1998:2).

Transnational advocacy networks differ from transnational social movements because of the nature of the network—issue-oriented, rather than "interpersonal social networks" (Tarrow 1996:24). Thus, these transnational advocacy networks may be sustained, but they are not integrated in the domestic social network system of the social movement.

Finally, transnational social movements are the most highly sustained transnational interaction with dense networks within the domestic social movement. A transnational social movement is "integrated within several societies, unified in its goals, and capable of sustained interaction with a variety of political authorities..." (1996:25). Tarrow does not deny this phenomenon, but cautions scholars to narrowly analyze transnational interactions in order to develop more precise conceptions of interactions between transnational actors and domestic actors.

Conceptions of networks, framing, and identity are significant in developing theories of transnational contentious collective action. Transnationally, *advocacy networks* may function as lines of communication; monetary and non-monetary resources; market access; information exchange and access; diplomatic and ideological support; leverage in institutional agenda-setting; and accountability of more powerful actors to act on specific policies.[20] Interpersonal, *social networks* refer to the "dense networks of communication and interaction" which link group members to group leaders. Thus, greater the communication and interaction among members leads to a higher degree of social networks. Social networks may be identified as the degree of social order within a group. They are impeded to the extent that there are factions and open conflict within the group.[21]

Yet, in transnational contentious collective action, *transnational networks*, meaning those networks among and between transnational and domestic groups, are significant in order to determine the level of transnational interaction and integration. In an attempt to flesh out the meaning of "integration in domestic networks" developed by Tarrow, transnational networks may be analyzed via two dimensions, the breadth of the networks and the depth of interpersonal networks and collective identity with each other. Drawing upon Stephen D. Krasner's (1988) institutional perspective of sovereignty, I refer to breadth as "the number of links" between transnational actors and domestic actors. Depth refers to the extent to which there are common identities and goals shared between and among the transnational and the domestic groups (Krasner 1998:77).[22] High levels of breadth and depth signify strong integration in transnational networks.

This builds upon the path breaking work of Tarrow, yet focuses on one more significant variable, *identity*. Common collective identities and goals separate those transnational networks that are present due to issue-only significance and those that are present due to a deeper held identity among actors. High levels of common identity and interpersonal links facilitate sustained interaction and integration.

Furthermore, the time frame aspect of Tarrow's topology does not specify how long actors must be involved in order to obtain the status of "sustained" social movements. Hypothetically, a transnational social movement organizes and mobilizes, yet achieves its goals and disbands. If a high level of integration was achieved and interaction was sustained for a short time-period (i.e., 6 months) with a "variety of political authorities," would this be a transnational social movement? Time is a significant variable and one that warrants further research. However, we must first under-

stand the links and interpersonal, social networks that exist among and
between transnational and domestic actors.

Intensity of Transnational Networks

Breadth ➤	Low	High
Depth ↓		
Low	Diffusion	Political Exchange
High	Transnational Issue Network	Transnational Social Movement

Based on this topology, we may categorize a truly transnational
social movement as one that is not only "integrated in several societies, unified in its goals, and capable of sustained interaction with a variety of political authorities," but also has common collective identities and purposes
(Tarrow 1996:22). Thus, transnational contentious collective action in its
most integrated form has high levels of breadth, or links among transnational and domestic actors, and high levels of depth, or embedded collective identities and common purposes.

My assumption of the significance of identity in collective action
draws upon Tilly's theory of organization: CATNESS X NETNESS =
ORGANIZATION (1978: 63). "Catness" characterizes the common identity of a group and "netness" characterizes the networks among group
members. A strong group organization implies high levels of catness and
netness, while a weak organization implies low levels.

This framework also extends the concept of identity beyond that of
class identity, which is argued by Alberto Melucci. It seeks to understand
identity outside of the North American or European concepts that have
largely shaped the literature on social movements. Melucci argues that
group identity is significant in the post-industrial society, such that in these
societies, individuals tend to act collectively to protect their own socio-economic situations, rather than to preserve common cultural identities
(1980:218–219). However, the situation of indigenous peoples in Latin
America differs from this perspective because their societies are pre-indus-

trial and community-based in many cases.

Myra Marx Ferree asserts that high levels of inter-dependence in pre-industrial communities create a level of community solidarity, unlike post-industrial, individualistic communities (1992: 8). In the case of Ecuador, indigenous peoples live together in groups and families and depend on one another and their environment for their survival. Their sense of identity extends beyond that of individual. Like Ferree, Mueller views actors as "socially embedded" in terms of group identities, which are rooted in social networks, particularly those based on gender, race, ethnicity, or religion (1992: 7). Moreover, shared grievances and expectations may also contribute to the formation of a collective identity. As the "discrepancy between people's value expectations and their value capabilities" increases, the possibility for conflict also increases[23]. Thus, an analysis of effective and sustained transnational contentious collective action must take into account the collective identity and grievances of the domestic group.

Gurr and Harff propose that the degree of ethnopolitical leadership and group cohesion are significant factors for the analysis of ethnopolitical conflict. They define "cohesive groups" as those "that have dense networks of communication and interaction linking leaders with followers. Cohesion within ethnic groups increases with increased communication and interaction" (1994:89). Therefore, more cohesive transnational contentious collective action would suggest the formation of transnational social movements.

In order to express these transnational collective identities, transnational social movements create *frames*. David A. Snow and his colleagues have presented the most influential work on framing and its role in the process of collective action. Doug McAdam summarizes framing, as developed by Snow and his colleagues, as "the conscious, strategic efforts of movement groups to fashion meaningful accounts of themselves and the issues at hand in order to motivate and legitimate their efforts" (1996:339). Frames convey the collective identity and common purposes of a social movement in a manner which attracts support from the broader public.

This support is garnered from the broader public via the use of symbols and ideas within the framing process. Anthony Oberschall (1996) argues that collective identity is narrated through a frame, which utilizes symbols within the political culture. Social movements scholars, such as Sidney Tarrow (1992) and Mayer N. Zald (1996), also assert that symbols used in the framing process are embedded within the political culture of a society. Snow (1988) refers to this influence of the broader public via frames as *frame resonance*. Through Tarrow's notion of cycles of protest, we know that "over time, a given collective action frame becomes part of the political culture—which is to say, part of the reservoir of symbols from which future movement entrepreneurs can choose" (1992:197).

The concept of *master frames* also provide insight to the links between framing processes and transnational contentious collective action. Snow and Benford conceive of master frames as "paradigms" to movement-specific frames (1992:138). Master frames provide a meaning which link smaller movement frames. Snow and Benford note that "Being more syntactically flexible and lexically universalistic than the restricted frame, the elaborated master frame allows for numerous aggrieved groups to tap it and elaborate their grievances in terms of its basic problem-solving schema" (1992:140). Master frames provide umbrellas under which organizers of transnational contentious collective action may choose symbols and utilize ideas that unite the various transnational and domestic actors involved.

For instance, the environmental movement is an example of a master frame which transnational advocacy networks and transnational social movements utilize to unite their collective identities and common purposes. Under the transnational environmental movement are many specific movement frames, such as safe waterways, rainforest protection, indigenous peoples, national park protection, and clean air. Yet, all of these frame-specific movements unite under the master frame umbrella of "the environment." Transnational advocacy networks and transnational social movements utilize symbols and already accepted ideas within the global civil society, such as human rights or the environment, and link them with the culturally-specific symbols of a domestic social movement. These links, or transnational networks, not only facilitate a united collective identity for the organizers, but also provide recognizable frames to the domestic society and the international society that they are seeking to influence. Furthermore, the issue-linkage of culturally specific frames to transnational frames allows resource-poor actors to transcend their specific locales and states to articulate their demands and initiate collective action on a transnational level.

Networks, framing, and identity are concepts that are not specific to domestic social movements alone. Networks provide linkages between transnational actors and domestic actors. These networks are created and sustained through collective identities and common purposes. The conveyance of these transnational collective identities, transnational advocacy networks, and transnational social movements is facilitated by the process of framing, which utilizes accepted symbols, already embedded in a political culture, to articulate meanings to a transnational audience. The process of globalization, fostered by an international state system, has developed symbols and ideas that transcend state boundaries. It is these transnational symbols and ideas which transnational advocacy network organizers and transnational social movement organizers utilize to unite the various domestic and transnational actors in order to influence political institutions on both a transnational and domestic level.

RESEARCH DESIGN

This study will utilize a comparative historical analysis of the Amazonian indigenous movement in order to demonstrate the impacts of transnational actors on domestic social movements and to distinguish between degrees of transnational contentious collective action. In no Amazonian country, does the Amazonian population exceed one percent of the total population. However, this small group in South America has gained substantial resources.

Although Ecuador's Amazonian population only totals approximately 120,000 people, or 1 percent of the country's population, this historically marginalized group has politically organized on a transnational level. While the Sierra and Coastal indigenous groups total over 37 percent of the total population and historically have been more integrated into the Ecuadorian society a level of transnational collective action strategies, nor have achieved the transnational level of political organization and resources that their Amazonian colleagues have gained. Thus, this study will focus on the Ecuadorian Amazon, including its plethora of ethnic groups, to understand why a region so small, with a diverse population that has been historically marginalized and excluded from the Ecuadorian political system, has been so successful in its collective action strategies and outcomes.

The first stage of this project focuses on the historical underpinnings of the transnational indigenous rights movement and its relationship to the transnational Amazonian indigenous movement. This section will elucidate historical precursors to the formation of the movement, and highlight important elements that precede transnational mobilization. The historical background and ethnic diversity of Ecuadorian society, outlining differences between the Sierra (or Highland) indigenous peoples and the Amazonian (or lowland) indigenous peoples will be briefly examined. This section will elucidate the indicators for the development of transnational advocacy networks.

It then proceeds to analyze the Amazonian indigenous movement and political organization prior to the democratization of Ecuador in 1979. This stage of research also highlights the pre-democratization developments of the petroleum industry in the Amazon and its initial contacts with indigenous populations. The purpose of this section of study is to understand the historical relationships between actors in the Amazon, Ecuadorian society, and the international system.

The second stage of research focuses on the post-democratization period of Ecuadorian history (1980 through 1999), when transnational contentious collective action increased in Ecuador. This section analyzes transnational advocacy networks and transnational social movements through case studies of five diverse Amazonian indigenous confederations and two Amazonian transnational social movement organizations (TSMOs). Not only does this second stage of research illustrate how and why transnational contentious collective action emerged in the post-democracy period, but it also develops a model of analysis of transnational networks and transnational social movements.

A comparison between Amazonian indigenous confederations and their varying degrees of transnational organization and mobilization provides information on the nature and sources of variation in transnational networks and how this affects policy outcomes. Furthermore, a study of Amazonian transnational social movement organizations demonstrates the differences between transnational networks and transnational social movements, while also enhancing our understanding of this complex process of mobilization and its outcomes on national and international levels.

The Amazonian confederations that are studied were chosen due to their variation in degrees of transnational collective activity, ethnic group in which they belong, and relation to the geographical and historical development of the petroleum industry. Thus, indigenous confederations have been chosen from Northern, Central and Southern provinces of the Amazon. This is significant in the sense that petroleum development in the Amazon began earlier in the Northern sections of the Amazon and is more recently developing in the South. The Amazonian confederations included in this study are: ONISE (Organization of Siona Indigenous Nationalities of Ecuador), OISE (Secoya Indigenous Organization of Ecuador), OPIP (Organization of Indigenous Peoples of Pastaza), FOISE (Federation of Indigenous Peoples of Sucumbíos), and the Cofánes. The Amazonian transnational social movement organizations considered in this study are: The Coalition for Amazonian Peoples and their Environment and COICA (The Coordinating Organization of Indigenous Peoples from the Amazon Basin). These indigenous organizations are analyzed in relation to their networks with the regional Amazonian organization (CONFENIAE), the national indigenous organization (CONAIE), and the transnational social movement organizations of COICA and the Coalitio employed in this research project. Twenty-five formal interviews and twenty-five informal interviews were conducted. These interviews focused primarily on indigenous, political, and INGO leaders involved in the transnational social movement organizations or the transnational advocacy networks. In addition to interviews, original, archival research was conducted in the offices of the INGOs involved in the process, indigenous confederation offices, and political, ministerial offices.

Secondary-resource research concentrated on academic studies from South American or Amazonian scholars. Most such studies and foundation working papers are only available in South America and permission is sometimes required to obtain copies. Although very little official government documentation exists on the subject of indigenous peoples in Ecuador, research in government offices was also conducted.

Aside from the above secondary resources, international relations and comparative politics studies on transnational social movements and transnational advocacy networks were utilized. Furthermore, this project draws quite heavily on the sociological literature of domestic social movements and the international political economy literature of MNCs in the international system.

Research for this project was conducted in a two- year period from June 1996 through June 1998. During that two-year time frame, primary research on Amazonian organizations was conducted in the capital city of Quito and in several Amazonian towns. The first year, sponsored by a doctoral research fellowship by the Institute for the Study of World Politics, centered on field-work with Amazonian indigenous leaders and other participants in the transnational advocacy networks. The second year of research focused primarily on the documents of South American researchers. The write-up of the project took place throughout the two year period and afterwards.

In addition to conventional research methodologies, I also received a Fulbright Fellowship for the study of the indigenous language, Quichua, in Ecuador during the summer of 1996. During that time, I lived in an indigenous village, learning the language and culture of the people. I also traveled frequently to indigenous protest events or organizational meetings. Therefore, participant-observation techniques were also utilized.

As is the case in any qualitative or quantitative research design, there are dangers of bias in case selection or analysis. However, this research project utilizes the largest number of case studies (seven in total) of Amazonian indigenous organizations possible to research in a limited time frame. Furthermore, very little research exists on transnational networks among Amazonian indigenous organizations, thus making the research process slightly longer than those of more established social movements.

The methodological tools utilized in this research project have been employed in a scientific manner. Moreover, interview questions were directed to the indicators identified in the previous discussion of hypotheses. The largest pool of interviews possible in a limited time frame within a lesser-developed country was conducted. Documented, archival information on transnational connections is difficult to obtain in indigenous confederations that tend to utilize verbal skills over written ones. Many times, indigenous leaders are leery of Western researchers and do not allow such privy information to be distributed in the first few sessions of interviews. Therefore, this process of the research was the most difficult to conduct. However, a large amount of archival material was obtained. Many times, INGO archives were better organized and more informative than were indigenous confederation archives.

Although bias in the research process is a constant concern, this research project has employed a diverse array of methodological tools to combat this problem. In addition, the ability to remain in Ecuador for two years not only provided more formal research time, but also a greater understanding of the culture surrounding the system of networks and its complex historical underpinnings. For this reason, historical processes as well as case study analysis are engaged in this research project.

NOTES

[1]See also, T.R. Gurr. (1994)."Peoples Against States: Ethnopolitical Conflict and the Changing World System." *International* 1993).Collective action is the joint action of a group in pursuit of common ends (Tilly 1978: 55). Thus, transnational collective action is the globalization of national collective action in which domestic actors and international actors pursue common ends through joint activities. See also Franke Wilmer, *The Indigenous Voice in World Politics* (Newbury Park: SAGE Publications.

[2] Rodolfo Stavenhagen also asserts that the indigenous movement in Latin America is a proactive movement, no longer reacting to state policy. He cites examples of indigenous mobilization on an international level through the Indigenous Working Group in the United Nations and the Declaration of Rights of Indigenous Peoples. These activities have challenged the nation-state systems of Latin America; (1984) "Los Movimientos Etnicos y el Estado Nacional en America Latina" *Desarollo: Una Publicacion de Colombia Para La America Latina.* Año XVIII #81.

[3]The commonly accepted definition of regimes is drawn from Krasner: "Regimes can be defined as sets of implicit or explicit principles, norms, rules, and decision-making procedures around which actors' expectations converge in a given area of

international relations" (1983. "Structural Causes and Regime Consequences: Regimes as Intervening Variables." in *International Regimes*. Ithaca: Cornell:2). Regimes possess a level of authority in the international system with regard to international cooperation and multilateral resolution of problems. However, the rise and decline of regimes, as well as their maintenance, has been attributed to states (Keohane 1989; Stein 1983). Although scholars have acknowledged the significance of norms (Hopkins and Puchala 1983; Young 1994) and networks of knowledge communities ("epistemic communities," Haas 1994), states are viewed as the key actors of authority within a regime.

[4]"Networks are forms of organization characterized by voluntary, reciprocal, and horizontal patterns of communication and exchange" (Keck and Sikkink 1998: 3). Walter Powell asserts that networks form when there is a need for "efficient, reliable information..." (1990. "Neither Market Nor Hierarchy: Network Forms of Organization," *Research in Organizational Behavior* 12:295–296).

[5]Keck and Sikkink (1998) define MNCs as different from other non-state actors because they have "instrumental goals," motivated by economic profit.

[6]See Keck and Sikkink 1998. Also, the notion of "purposive" was personally communicated to me by Alison Brysk.

[7]Jack Donnelly (1994) argues that the international human rights movement has changed national sovereignty of states by permitting individuals to seek aid on an international level. Kathryn Sikkink (1994) asserts that human rights NGOs played a crucial role in changing human rights policies within states. Finally, Kal Raustiala (1994) demonstrates the flow of information between NGOs, societal forces, and states with regard to environmental policies. He cites the formal and informal roles of environmental NGOs on both the domestic and international levels.

[8]On the concept of "master frames," see Tarrow, *Power in Movement,* p. 131; and Snow and Benford in Bert Klandermans, et. al., eds. *From Structure to Action: Comparing Social Movement Research Across Cultures* (Greenwich,CT:JAI Press, 1988), p.199.

[9]Thoughts on this subject are derived from Virginia Haufler (1996). "Private International Regimes and Corporate Norms." Paper Presented at the Workshop on "Private Power, Public Power, and International Regimes," April 16, 1996, San Diego, California.

[10] Deborah Yashar notes that recent state reforms in Latin America have made the state "less capable" of acting as a "political authority in rural areas" (1998:33).

[11]See also, D. McAdam and D. Rucht (1993). McAdam and Rucht analyze the cross-national diffusion of movements by identifying channels of information exchange between actors involved in the movements. They identify four channels: 1)people who transmit the information; 2)people who accept the information; 3) items or information that is diffused; and 4) people, media, or organizations which foster a "channel of diffusion" (1993:59). In this framework, the channels of dif-

fusion for information exchange are identified as transnational actors and societal actors.

[12]This may include participation in negotiation processes between state officials and indigenous leaders; the creation of new institutions which represent indigenous needs; and a dialogue which includes indigenous leaders in the formation of new state or local policies pertaining to indigenous groups.

[13]This may include participation in negotiation processes between state officials and transnational actors; the creation of new institutions which represent indigenous needs, or the alteration of prior institutions to include their needs; and a dialogue, or discourse which includes indigenous leaders in the formation of new policies pertaining to their ethnic groups.

[14]Alison Brysk and Carol Wise also argue that economic adjustment policies impact ethnic conflict, particularly in states that increase political and economic liberalization, but remove channels for popular participation. (1995). "Economic Adjustment and Ethnic Conflict in Bolivia, Mexico, and Peru." Paper presented ate the *International Studies Association Meeting*, Chicago, IL, February 21–25, 1995.

[15]*Levantamiento* is best translated as an uprising. This refers to organized demonstrations and protests.

[16]See also, J. Kane (1995). *Savages*. New York. Knopf Publishers.

[17] T.R. Gurr denotes indigenous peoples as a sub-group of "ethno-national peoples, who were historically autonomous and who have pursued separatist objectives at some time in the last fifty years." Indigenous peoples are cross classified as ethno-nationalists. They are characterized as those people who live in "peripheral and inaccessible mountain valleys, tropical rainforests, steppes, or deserts, ... until quite recently." Their primary concerns are autonomy issues and they are culturally distinct from groups that live in city centers or from the colonial authority. (1993:20)

[18]For further explanation of the rational choice perspective on collective action, see M. Olson (1965); R. Hardin (1982); D. Chong (1991); and M. Lichbach (1994).

[19] These ideas are derived from: Tarrow, Sidney. "Imagined Commonalities: The Puzzle of Transnational Civic Activism," a talk delivered at the Princeton University Department of Politics and Rutger's University Department of Political Science, December 5 and 6, 1996.

[20] My ideas on this subject derive from various works including, Gurr 1994:Revised Minorities at Risk Code Sheet; Gurr and Harff 1994; Keck and Sikkink 1998; Smith 1996; and Tarrow 1996.

[21] My ideas on social networks derive from the work of Gurr and Harff 1994.

[22]My thanks to John D. Occhipinti for pointing this article out to me in a personal communication.

[23]T.R. Gurr. (1970). *Why Men Rebel*. Princeton: Princeton University Press:13.

CHAPTER THREE

Historical Precursors

THIS CHAPTER WILL EXAMINE THE HISTORY OF THE TRANSNATIONAL indigenous rights movement and the indigenous movement in Ecuador, and the dynamic relationship between the two. It will also set the foundations for the later analysis of the Ecuadorian transnational indigenous movement and the Amazonian transnational indigenous movement. It is important to examine the historical underpinnings of transnational contentious politics in order to understand its roots and to be able to predict, based on previous indicators, its effectiveness. Thus, this portion of the research project will demonstrate the motives for transnational contentious politics and analyze the historical backdrop and connections between Ecuador, the Amazonian region, and the transnational indigenous rights movement.

The historical events prior to the formation of transnational Amazonian movements indicate a lack of national resources, a lack of representation on national levels, and an increase of transnational actors in the Amazonian region. Moreover, they trace the formation of framing techniques and strategies over the years. Much of the recent literature on transnational advocacy networks and social movements focuses on the recent, global impacts due to new technologies and abilities to communicate. However, this chapter intends to expand the research designs of transnational contentious politics to include their historical precursors and link them to current organization and mobilization strategies.[1]

THE HISTORY OF THE TRANSNATIONAL INDIGENOUS
RIGHTS MOVEMENT

As Stefano Varese notes, a transnational network of indigenous peoples from North and South America has been forming over the past three decades (1996:16). These transnational networks include indigenous and non-indigenous actors from social sectors within states, international organizations, and multinational corporations. A common factor among actors within these networks is their identification with an ethnic group, such as Quichua, Quechua, Aymara, Shuar, etc. Moreover, Varese argues that the unrepresentative nature of the Latin American state has fueled mobilization on transnational levels from communal, indigenous groups (1996:23). One of the outcomes of this transnational mobilization is the change in international discourse and ideas, which is illustrated by the inclusion of indigenous peoples in international organizations, such as the United Nations, the International Labor Organization, and the Organization of American States, and the granting of international funds to development projects located in indigenous territories from international funding agencies, such as The World Bank (1996:24).

In addition to ideational change, there has been an institutionalization of indigenous rights organizations in the structure of international organizations. Some scholars argue that the reason for organization and mobilization on a transnational level for indigenous peoples is the role of the state as participant in international liberal economic policies, which highlights industrialization and technology, thus excluding large portions of the agrarian, indigenous populations of the Americas.[2] In conjunction with these liberal economic policies, the spread of transnational corporations (TNCs) was occurring in much of the Third World, and particularly in areas with indigenous populations (Bice 1996:18–19, Wilmer 1993: 128–129). Therefore, indigenous peoples, in many respects, have moved to the transnational level as a "last resort" to obtain representation for their demands and sovereignty over their traditional lands.

The transnational indigenous movement began in the North with U.S.-and-Canada-based international indigenous organizations. In 1968, the National Indian Brotherhood (NIB) formed in Canada. Beginning in 1971, its president George Manuel organized international meetings with indigenous representatives from Latin America, Scandinavia, and the U.S. By 1975, these organizational meetings had developed into the World Council of Indigenous Peoples (WCIP), representing the U.S., Canada, South America, Europe-Greenland, and the South Pacific. This organization and a later offshoot of it, the International Indian Treaty Council

(IITC), mobilized the first transnational activities of the movement (Maiguashca 1996:26–27).

Furthermore, anthropologists became active in the struggle. A Norwegian anthropologist, Helge Kleivan, founded the International Work Group for Indigenous Affairs (IWGIA), in 1968, which focuses on human rights and the ability of indigenous peoples to maintain their traditional forms of living (Maiguashca 1996: 28). In 1972, a Harvard anthropologist, David Maybury, founded Cultural Survival, which is one of the most prominent activist organizations for indigenous peoples in the U.S., and produces research projects as well as a quarterly magazine, also named *Cultural Survival.*

In addition to activist groups, the Protestant Church became highly involved in the indigenous movement beginning in 1971 and throughout the 1980s. The World Council of Churches (W.C.C.), a Protestant organization for all denominations, initiated meetings among Latin American indigenous leaders to discuss inter-ethnic conflict in Latin America. The first of two conferences was held in January 1971, in Barbados, and was followed by another in July 1977. The purpose of these conferences was interaction between anthropologists and indigenous leaders (Maiguashca 1996:28). Although such contacts were developed, the conference primarily sparked communication networks among indigenous leaders. It was also in Barbados that Amazonian indigenous leaders formulated the initial plans for a pan Amazonian organization that would later be the Coordinator of Indigenous Organizations of the Amazon Basin (COICA).

While the WCIP continued to develop its transnational links, seven other transnational indigenous organizations formed and achieve consultative status within the United Nations[3]. In 1982, through the leadership of the IITC, the UN Working Group on Indigenous Populations was established. This specialized group within the UN represented the concerns of indigenous peoples from all over the world via the networks of the original eight consultative status member-organizations. The majority of the transnational indigenous organizations were North America-based. However, the Indian Law Resource Center (ILRC), founded in 1978, expanded its work to represent the legal claims of indigenous peoples in Latin America in the mid-1980s. By the late-1980s, the Amazonian transnational organization had also received consultative status within the United Nations, which inspired many more transnational networks and information exchanges among indigenous groups.[4]

During the same time period, Amazonian leaders of state were organizing on a pan Amazonian level to coordinate policies and strategies among their countries. In July 1978, the Amazonian Cooperation Treaty

(ACT) was signed by Brazil, Bolivia, Colombia, Ecuador, Guyana, Peru, Surinam, and Venezuela. This treaty commissioned coordination among Amazonian-country presidents to preserve the environment and coordinate policies that impact Amazonian areas (Kremling Gómez 1997:22–23). This treaty also included the participation of various transnational actors, such as the Food and Agriculture Organization of the UN, the Inter-American Development Bank, the World Bank, and various international non-governmental organizations. The ACT functioned as a catalyst of communication between Amazonian-state and non-state leaders. Therefore, Amazonian indigenous confederations became gradually more exposed to the transnational funding agencies for development projects in their region. These networks initiated further Amazonian organizational integration and communication.

Amazonian countries in South America had been experiencing similar development dilemmas, which created another common variable for the organization of indigenous peoples. During the 1970s, new technologies made it possible to extract minerals from the Amazonian subsoil. With this development, "colonos," or colonists, from other regions of these countries moved to the Amazonian regions due to employment prospects. Moreover, transnational mineral and petroleum companies began seismic testing and drilling in these once sparsely inhabited areas. The development and extraction of palm oil, wood, petroleum, precious metals, such as gold, and rubber were not only bases for economic development for South American countries, but also bases for payment of the international debts which they would accumulate during the late 1970s and into the 1980s (Zárate B. 1993: 23–33). Thus, the social, economic, and ecological configuration of the Amazon had changed, which caused a change in not only domestic organization, but also transnational organization.

During the mid to late-1980s, Amazonian indigenous leaders began to meet among themselves, without the aid of missionary organizations or state actors as interlocutors. Their organization became more political, yet was based on a common, historical vision shared by indigenous peoples. The Coordinator of Indigenous Organizations of the Amazon Basin, or COICA, which will be discussed later in this project, was founded in 1984, and became the transnational movement organization (TSMO) for the pan Amazonian movement. COICA, while funded by international organizations such as the Inter-American Foundation (IAF), Oxfam America, and IBIS Denmark, remains autonomous in its activities and retains a strong common identity among its members.

It was also during this time period that framing strategies developed. Indigenous peoples came to portray themselves as part of a larger cosmovision of the planet. They were actors and integral parts of their surrounding eco-system, which in turn, was part of the larger world ecological system. They had placed themselves within the "green" agenda of other transnational actors, while at the same time including indigenous cultures and traditions within the frame. Therefore, according to their master frame, the Amazon was the lungs of the Earth and the indigenous populations were its caretakers.

The transnational movement of indigenous peoples is composed of various transnational networks and movement organizations that coordinate policies and create new avenues for collective action. Indigenous peoples have moved their mobilization strategies from the floors of national Congresses and Parliaments to the floors of the United Nations and other international organizations. Moreover, they have created new opportunity structures in which they can formulate policy and obtain resources. The Amazonian transnational movement operates within the larger umbrella of the transnational indigenous movement, while also creating venues for its own demands and concerns. The following section of this chapter will analyze the particular history of one Amazonian country, Ecuador, and the complex set of networks between Ecuadorian indigenous peoples and the transnational Amazonian movement.

THE DEVELOPMENT OF THE INDIGENOUS ORGANIZATION IN ECUADOR

The indigenous movement in Ecuador has mobilized on local, regional, national, and international levels and is increasingly engaged in negotiations with the Ecuadorian government. The indigenous population is estimated from 15 percent to 40 percent of the population, yet 37 percent is the percentage most often cited. Ecuador contains one of the largest and most diverse indigenous populations in the Americas.[5] Although indigenous peoples in Ecuador, and throughout the Andean region, have been organized since the time of the Incas and have a history of political unrest dating back to colonial times, recent technological advancements and influx of transnational actors to the country have changed their mobilization strategies. Since the Indian uprising in 1990, Ecuador has had many organized indigenous protests against government and international policies[6]. This section will focus primarily on the development of the transnational networks of the Ecuadorian indigenous movement through the most recent 1993–1994 uprisings and the current time period as an illustration of the transnational mobilization of an Amazonian indigenous group.

Ecuador's indigenous groups are organized on local, regional, and national levels. A primary motivator for multi-level organization was the

1964 Agrarian Reform Laws promulgated under the military dictatorship of General Rodriguez Lara. These laws promoted the colonization of the Amazonian region under the guidance of the Ecuadorian Institute for Agrarian Reform and Colonization (IERAC). Much of this colonized land was traditionally inhabited by indigenous communities. Moreover, the oil boom in the 1970s further eroded the land on which indigenous communities had dwelled (Selverston 1994: 135).

The indigenous movement in Ecuador is not a class based or ideologically based struggle. It is composed of various indigenous groups, which associate the movement with cultural discrimination, not class discrimination. One distinction that these groups make is their social status (regardless of class status) is far lower than the social status of a non-Indian. Although many social movements in Latin America in the past have been linked with Leftist ideology or mobilization tactics, these groups are not aligned with any particular political ideology or party. Instead, they call for a reformulation of the political and social structure in order to include their interests and needs.

In 1964, under the guidance of missionary groups, the first Indian federation was founded, called the Federation of the Shuar Centers. This group of Ecuadorian Indians established programs for their communities apart from state programs. These programs included bilingual education, health, and cattle ranching. They organized in response to the colonization of the land which they claimed as home in the Amazon. By the mid-1970s, the Shuar Federation broke its ties with missionary groups in order to develop a policy-oriented organization without religious affiliations.

Following the Shuar Federation, the Organization of the People of Pastaza (OPIP) and the Federation of the Indigenous Organization of Napo (FOIN) formed. These were provincial indigenous organizations throughout the Amazonian region. They synthesized the Indian tradition of shamanism with the more western forms of organization, such as a president, a vice-president, and a secretary. These groups were primarily concerned with a struggle to protect their land (136).

In 1980, the groups of the Amazon joined together to form the Confederation of Indigenous Nationalities of the Ecuadorian Amazon (CONFENIAE). This regional organization contained members of the Shuar and Quichua Indians in leadership positions, in addition to other Amazonian ethnic group-members of the Achuar, Huaoroni, Cofán, Siona, and Secoya tribes. The decision-making body of the CONFENIAE is the Congress which is held every two years. Through this alliance, the organization has brought their issues to the public attention and to the political agendas of national and international groups. It has formed alliances with environmental and human rights organizations, in addition to "bringing oil companies and the government to the negotiating table, particularly regarding development practices in the Amazon" (136).

Moreover, the regional association has also struggled for land rights. In 1991, large tracts of land were awarded to the Huaorani people (the largest land grant in the Amazonian region) in response to a massive demonstration by over three thousand indigenous people. This demonstration was aided by other Indian groups not included in the CONFENIAE (137).

Like their Amazonian allies, the Sierra regional indigenous groups organized primarily in response to harsh agrarian land reforms in the 1960s. These groups were originally organized by the Ecuadorian Communist Party in 1944, which established the Ecuadorian Indigenous Federation (FEI). However, due to land re-distribution into small parcels shared among indigenous communities and the limited access of funds for agro-industrial technology for indigenous peoples, the FEI organized many protests against the government policy of agrarian reform. In addition to its original influence by communists, the FEI was also aided by the Catholic Church. In 1972, the Catholic Church sponsored the first regional meeting of the Sierra Indian communities, which established ECUARUNARI (Ecuador Runacunapac Riccharimui). At first, the church was the leading force in this organization. However, ECUARUNARI has since abandoned the goals of the church and functions now as a federation of local Indian communities (138–139).

While both the Sierra and Amazonian indigenous peoples are organized politically and socially, they are two unique cases with differing forms of relations within the state and outside of the state. The Amazon, due to its difficult terrain and remoteness, was explored by Spanish conquistadores later than the Sierra portions of the country. This greatly impacted relations between indigenous and non-indigenous peoples in both regions. The Sierra has traditionally had an agricultural and textile based economy, while the land in the Amazon was utilized very little for national agriculture.

A clear example of the historical difference between these two regions is the 1861 Constitution, which stated that "The Eastern province will be governed by special laws until its population grows and the progression of its civilization allow it to govern itself like the rest of the country" (Restrepo G. 1993:153). This statement illustrates the lack of knowledge of the region, assuming that only a small population lived there, even though over 350,000 indigenous peoples lived there during this time-period. Furthermore, it indicates a lack of acceptance of the Amazonian indigenous cultures and traditions so much so that it relegates the region to special government status until it "advances."

The current Constitution of 1978 still singles out the Amazon as a "special region," but does not treat it differently in terms of inclusion within the national governmental system. Thus, the Amazon has historically remained relatively separate from the rest of the state and far more resource impoverished due to lack of transportation, technology, communication networks, and trade of goods. Even though the Amazon has remained quite distant from national political inclusion, unlike the Sierra indigenous peoples, it has managed, via transnational advocacy networks, to increase its resource pool and utilize transnational mobilization strategies to successfully influence national and transnational policy outcomes.[7]

While there are great historical and prevailing differences between the two regions, both are organized on a national level within one organization. The national Indian organization of Ecuador is CONAIE. It was first formed through the union of ECUARUNARI and CONFENIAE in 1980 and originally called the Coordinating Council of Indigenous Nationalities of Ecuador (CONACNIE). Following this union, the coastal Indian communities formed a regional group, COICE (Coordinator of Indigenous Organizations of the Coast of Ecuador), and it joined the two former groups to form the current day CONAIE.

CONAIE has a president, vice-president, and secretaries for various issue areas, such as human rights, women, health, and education. Its permanent office is in Quito and it has representatives from each Indian group organized at congressional and assembly levels. CONAIE is very structured and its facilities are not primitive at all. They utilize all media publications and communication tools, such as computers, fax machines, cellular phones, etc. Thus, they are highly organized and connected to each region in order to ensure quick and facile mobilization. Furthermore, their resources derive from various international organizations including anthropological groups, environmental organizations, OXFAM AMERICA, the Inter-American Foundation (IAF), and Rainforest Action Network (RAN), in addition to various community support organizations (Selverston 1995:140). CONAIE is organized at local, regional, national, and international levels. All of these levels aid in its ability to gain resources and to mobilize effectively.

As the national representative for the indigenous peoples of Ecuador, CONAIE has a set of sixteen goals. These include demands to end the "subjugation of indigenous peoples," land distribution and economic development, investment in the infrastructure and the removal of barriers put in place by the state to impede indigenous economic development (such as debt, lack of credit, regressive taxation, and a price structure biased against indian products), cultural rights for bilingual education, control of indigenous archeological sites, and government support for native medicine. Furthermore, the indigenous groups call for Ecuador to be recognized as a "plurinational, multi-ethnic" state (Field 1991: 40).

In the Fourth Congress of CONAIE, in December 1993, the group devised resolutions for its further organization and management. Regional parliaments were created with the intention of unification into a National Parliament in the near future. An Annual Fund was created as part of the resources for the mobilization of the group in response to land and territorial conflicts. A bank was established in order to aid small, indigenous farmers with debts. Special programs and funds were created to support Amazonian indigenous peoples in their negotiations with multinational oil companies. One such example, which will be further analyzed later in this project, is the lawsuit of the Cofán Indians against Texaco Oil Company for damaging their lands with oil spills and creating health hazards. Finally, CONAIE committed its support to the work of the United Nations in its "Declaration of the Decade for Indigenous Peoples" (Cuarto Congreso De La CONAIE Mantiene Indpendencia de Partidos Politicos). Thus, the Congress of the CONAIE establishes regional, national, and international goals to achieve.

The demands made by CONAIE are in response to the discrimination and repressive policies of the state toward indigenous communities. For example, COMUNIDEC (a not-for-profit organization that manages grassroots development projects for international organizations) reports that 70–80 percent of the funding for indigenous communities is funneled through a system of state bureaucracies rather than being managed by indigenous communities and leaders. These programs are also not implemented with the consultation of the indigenous communities for which they are established. Moreover, *El Comercio* (a national Ecuadorian newspaper) reports that barely 1 percent of the economic budget for Ecuador is spent on the indigenous populations (Van Cott 1994, *The Journal of Commerce*). Based on these figures and the high degree of social stigma against indigenous individuals as well as their lack of political participation, these groups and individuals have high levels of deprivation.[8] Also, their resources, organization, communication networks, mobilization, and common norms and justifications afford CONAIE high levels of group cohesion and identity. Yet, as will be further examined, these variables of group discrimination, deprivation, identity, and cohesion are symbiotically affected by transnational actors and organizations, which in turn have highly varied relationships with the Sierra and Amazonian regional groups.

THE ROLE OF THE STATE

As noted in the previous chapter, one of the factors that influences organization transnationally is a lack of representation and resources on a national level. In the case of Ecuador, as is the case in many Amazonian countries, indigenous groups have been isolated from the political process of the country. Therefore, leaders of these movements circumvented the state and found openings in the international political arena.

As Amparo Menéndez-Carrion (1989) and Catherine Conaghan (1995) note, Ecuador's political system, both historically as well as currently, suffers from a lack of representation of its diverse population. This lack of representation is observed through various factors, including: an unstable, multi-party system; an ethnically diverse society; a fragmented electorate; a long history of "patronazgo," or patron-client relations; and strong external influences upon state institutions. All of these factors contribute to closure of venues of opportunity for actors in social movements, forcing them to look beyond the borders of states to mobilize.

Prior to 1978, Ecuador was governed by military rule. However, since its transition to democracy in 1979, it has been developing a modern party system, which continues to be unstable. Twenty-three political parties have legal status, not including various other movements attempting to obtain legal status. The party system stems from pre-democratic, "hacendado" times when the primarily landowning class governed the country (Conaghan 1995:435–439). The political parties are characteristically dominated by upper to upper-middle class individuals from landowning families. Until the foundation of Pachakutik in 1996, a political party with indigenous members, indigenous peoples had very few interactions within the national party system. Thus, party institutions were not a viable means of mobilization for the indigenous movement of Ecuador.

The ethnic diversity of Ecuador and its social fragmentation also contribute to the difficulties of achieving a united electorate. Ecuador has at least twelve distinct indigenous communities, composing over thirty-seven percent of the total population, and an Afro-Ecuadorian community of between five and six percent of the total population. Moreover, there are great regional differences in the country among the coast, the Sierra, the Amazon, and the Galapagos. In every election since 1978, the country has witnessed great divides on voting between the coast and the Sierra. These regional differences also exist among indigenous communities, which speak different languages and do not share the same customs and traditions, depending on their region (Menéndez-Carrion 1989: 18). Thus, within the CONAIE, indigenous leaders from the Amazon and the Sierra are often divided on issue-areas. This diversity of ethnicity, regionalism, and classes causes fragmentation not only in the electorate, but also within movements.

Furthermore, there is a long history (since the Seventeenth Century) of "latifundio," or large landowning classes that dominated the Sierra and the coast and founded large haciendas for the production of agricultural goods and textiles, utilizing inexpensive, indigenous labor. This system was less prevalent in the Amazon due to the minimal conquest of these lands by the Spanish. The "latifundio" system was the main base of the Ecuadorian economy until the mid-1960s and to a minor extent continues to function on various, historic haciendas. This system created a society of "patrones" who were the landowners, and workers, who were primarily indigenous communities. These workers were dependent upon the "patrón" for food, clothing, shelter, work, health care, and daily needs. "Patrones," in return for providing these goods, expected long hours of labor and production on their land, rights to which were granted to them by the Spanish royalty (Ayala Mora 1993: 47–48). For this reason, indigenous communities, particularly in the Sierra, had very little political organization outside of their respective haciendas. Thus, "patronazgo" is another form of historical closure to political institutions which the indigenous communities faced.

While domestic factors were significant, both historically and more recently, transnational variables also impacted the ability of the Ecuadorian state to respond to indigenous demands. From the time of the conquest to 1830, Ecuador was penetrated by external, transnational actors. The colonial period was the beginning of the opening of Ecuador to outside, transnational actors, namely, the Spanish royalty and its administration. However, the end of colonialism brought the "latifundio" system, which allowed the Spanish vice-royalty (now settled in Ecuador) to extend its control over the indigenous communities, particularly in the Sierra. The Agrarian Land Reform ended this system through the division of agricultural land into parcels and gave them to indigenous communities for their own development. However, by 1972, the state had again opened itself to outside influence with the sale of blocks in the Amazon for oil production. During the military rule of General Rodriguez Lara (1972–1976), petroleum production accounted for over seventy percent of the national budget (Interview May 12, 1998) . From that point on, the Ecuadorian Amazon and national governmental institutions have been strongly influenced by oil production and oil company executives. These external influences, which favored industrialization and liberal economic policies, greatly affected the traditional, agricultural economy of indigenous communities. Thus, indigenous actors, particularly from the Amazon, who were not consulted on any policy changes in their region, were motivated to create transnational policy openings where national ones did not exist.

PRE-DEMOCRATIC ECUADOR

The Ecuadorian state was founded on the 13th of May 1830, and its first President, General Juan José Flores, initiated a constituent assembly as its first government institution. Ecuador has reformed its governmental constitution eighteen times, with the most recent being in 1978, which suspended the literacy requirement for voting that had been in effect since its inception. The pre-democratic history of Ecuador is one of landowning classes and military leaders who dominated Ecuador's landscape since colonial times. Most early leaders of the country were cacao plantation owners, interested in the consolidation of land and increased export. During the late-1800s and early 1900s, their principal political protagonists were leaders of the Catholic Church and their "liberal" opponents. These leaders usually assumed state control via a military coup. Thus, elections rarely took place and even so, the majority of indigenous peoples were not able to vote, either because of lack of information or illiteracy.

In 1960, President Velasco Ibarra won office as a populist and leader of the poor. However, he was overthrown the following year by a military junta that remained in power until the transition to democracy in 1979. Although the pre-democratic period had various populist leaders, these leaders were generally supported by worker's unions and were of a leftist ideology. No influence by indigenous leaders in the national political system is observed until the initiation of indigenous confederations in the late 1970s and the first indigenous uprising in 1990 (Ayala Mora 1993:93–107).[9] Based on this history, the pre-democratic, hacienda system did not provide indigenous peoples with the political space for organization and representation of their demands.

THE TRANSITION TO DEMOCRACY

It is clear, based on the evolution of governmental policies, that the state is attempting to modernize its society through liberal economic policies. As Selverston posits, much of government policy is based on modernization, "a project that involves the creation of a strong national identity and the acculturation of native peoples into the dominant social and economic culture" (Selverston 1994: 143). However, the demands of the indigenous groups in Ecuador do not support the policies of inclusion and assimilation, but rather they favor policies that allow them to pursue their own economic, political, and cultural needs and traditions. This divergence in agendas has created tension between the state and the indigenous communities.

In 1979, Ecuador democratized with the election of the Roldós-Hurtado administration (1979–1984). Roldós was elected as the "people's president," obtaining votes from much of Ecuador's poor and illiterate. He even gave part of his acceptance speech in Quichua. He created the Center for the Study of Indigenous Education (CIEI), which facilitated literacy and bilingual education programs. Furthermore, he established the National Office for Indigenous Affairs in the Ministry of Social Welfare. However, indigenous groups criticized the "paternalism" of this office.

During the following two presidential administrations (until 1988), of Hurtado and Febres Cordero, indigenous groups expressed continued dissatisfaction with the policies of the government. This time-period also coincides with IMF economic reforms, which favored outside investment into the country and agro-industrial development. These reforms, particularly during the Febres Cordero administration, caused a decline in traditional agriculture, in addition to a dependence upon petroleum profits. Therefore, economic deprivation increased during this period, whereas indigenous political participation in the government remained minimal. This spurred increasing levels of deprivation that were manifested through public protest in 1982 from union, agricultural, and indigenous sectors. Reports from NGOs (such as Oxfam America) and research organizations (such as COMUNIDEC) note that repressive measures were utilized during this period, including military force against agrarian, or "campesino," protestors; the burning of indigenous homes; and kidnappings (Ibarra 1992: 181; Salacuse 1993). However, there are no governmental documents, nor official news sources to verify these accounts.

At the time of the Hurtado and Febres Cordero administrations, Ecuador was undergoing international debt negotiations as well. During the majority of the 1980s, Ecuador's trade and debt became even more dependent upon the United States. For example, in 1985, 57.1 percent of Ecuador's exports and 35.1 percent of imports were traded with the United States. Also, in 1985, Ecuador's petroleum revenues accounted for 59.8 percent of the total budget revenues for the state, yet its income was reduced by one half at this time due to a world decrease in oil prices. Ecuador was not only dependent on the US for trade, but also for loans, of which the US had given Ecuador over $55.5 million from 1984—1987. Aside from the US direct aid, the IMF and the World Bank aided the Ecuadorian government. By 1987, Ecuador's external debt exceeded $10 billion, over 60 percent being owed to US private banks (Hey 1993: 553–554). Thus, Ecuador, under the administrations of Hurtado and Febres Cordero was dependent upon many Northern modernization policies in order to halt its economic crisis. This international debt crisis contributed to the lack of social programs, particularly those directed at indigenous development and aid.

In 1988, President Rodrigo Borja was elected. Although his administration provided more social programs for indigenous communities than the previous two, indigenous mobilization had increased in response to the previous lack of participation in the national social and economic systems. Borja did create a commission for indigenous concerns, which focused primarily on education, territory, and legitimacy of indigenous needs. One way in which Borja tried to give legitimacy to the Indians was by recognizing CONAIE as the representative of the indigenous communities of Ecuador. While this recognition was merely symbolic, it did provide CONAIE with the legitimacy and attention to enter negotiations and concessions after the 1990 uprising of indigenous groups, organized by CONAIE (Selverston 1994: 145).

THE 1990 UPRISING

On May 27, 1990, 160 CONAIE activists occupied the Santo Domingo Cathedral in Quito and demanded immediate resolution of land disputes in six Sierra highland provinces. The next day, one thousand Indians representing approximately 70 organizations marched to Quito and presented President Borja with a 16 point petition, which included legalization of territories, respect for agrarian reform law, funds for bilingual education, and amending the Constitution to declare Ecuador a multinational state.

During the following week, the country witnessed "levantamientos," or uprisings in the Sierra provinces of Bolívar, Chimborazo, Cotopaxi, Tungurahua, Pinchincha, and Imbabura. In the province of Bolívar, 5,000 Indians demonstrated and seized the capital. In Guaranda, indigenous peoples cut off the water supply and blocked roads. In each of these provinces, Indian-run food markets were also closed down, causing a food shortage. The Indians covered the roads with large boulders, cutting off transportation and food supply, which demonstrated the country's dependence upon native farmers. Moreover, in the province of Chimborazo, MICH (the Indigenous Movement of Chimborazo), held the governor and local police hostage. In Cotopaxi, indigenous farmers expelled hacendados from the land that they traditionally had farmed. Overall, the protests organized by CONAIE shut down the country of Ecuador for over one week (Van Cott 1993: 44; Field 1991: 39; Salacuse 1993: 37).

One important factor in the organization of the 1990 uprising, or protest, was the amount of support from sectors of civil society, including many "campesino" and union non-Indian organizations and international organizations. Many students, laborers, and the Church aided in the protest, either through protest participation or support for the indigenous groups. Non-governmental organizations, such as OXFAM and others, provided resources for the mobilization of the CONAIE (Salacuse 1993: 37).

In response to this protest, the Ecuadorian government deployed national police and the army to the Sierra provinces. Guns, tanks, and tear gas were utilized to halt the protestors. In a violent struggle, the MICH leader, Oswaldo Cuwi, was killed by the police (Field 1991: 39). Military forces also surrounded the Santo Domingo Cathedral in Quito. At first, violence was the means used by the government under Borja to control this uprising.

However, in response to international pressures, on June 8, 1990, President Borja appointed several upper level ministers, including the head of the Agrarian Reform Ministry (IERAC), to negotiate with the indigenous groups. The Archbishop of Quito acted as the mediator and Luís Macas (then vicepresident of CONAIE, later elected to the National Congress) was the Indian spokesperson. Eleven days later, the Indians left the Cathedral peacefully. (Salacuse 1993: 38; Field 1991: 40). In response to these negotiations, bilingual education was restored and an Indigenous Affairs Office was established. Moreover, through the indigenous mobilization on a transnational level, some indigenous demands were met and transnational networks increased.

Further incidents and uprisings by indigenous groups were treated more seriously and negotiations began promptly. For example, in April 1992, representatives of OPIP (The Organization of Indigenous Peoples of Pastaza, in the Amazon) marched to Quito and demanded control of their ancestral land in the rainforest. President Borja, in return, met with 100 indigenous leaders. After some time, the Indians of Pastaza were granted the legal title of three million acres of homelands. This was the largest land grant yet made to Ecuadorian Indians (Salacuse 1993: 39–40).

In addition, in August 1991, CONAIE occupied the national legislature, demanding talks between the government and the Indians. By mid-1992, seven of the fifteen land disputes were settled through indigenous and governmental negotiations. Finally, in 1992 (the 500th Anniversary of the Conquest), CONAIE organized an electoral boycott, which meant a boycott of over two million Ecuadorian voters of the six million total. This boycott, however, halted when indigenous leaders from CONAIE ran for office in leftist political parties (Van Cott 1993: 44). Through the organization of CONAIE and its member groups, power relationships in Ecuador have been re-distributed, such that Indian concerns can no longer be ignored by the government.

This re-distribution of power does not end at the national level, though, because the organization and resources of CONAIE and other Indian groups derive largely from external, international forces, such as the United Nations Working Group for Indigenous Peoples, and other non-governmental organizations. Moreover, the international economic system played a role in the 1990 uprising. Between 1987 and 1991, real salaries declined in Ecuador 10 per cent annually, while prices of oil increased 50 per cent (Ortiz 1994: 8). This increased the already great disparity between the poor and the wealthy. Indeed, the indigenous groups were the hardest hit. Thus, the indigenous mobilization has given a voice to the many other silent Ecuadorians and has altered the relationship between the national and international systems.

This tripartite interdependence among the international, national, and group levels increased under the administration of Sixto Durán Ballen (elected in 1992). Durán attempted to rescind the bilingual education agreement negotiated with CONAIE and Borja, but did not due to mass protest. Duran did open an indigenous office in the national government and named an Otavalo Indian and indigenous intellectual, José Quimbo, to the position. However, the office has very little funding and is now rejected by CONAIE. Due to a stalemate on negotiations of land reforms in Yuracruz (the land has been awarded to the indigenies, but without funding), hacendados (land owners) hired security officers to protect them from the sometimes violent protests and demonstrations of Indians in that area. These protests and demonstrations included hailing stones and rocks at cars; burning tires in the road or in front of hacendado homes; stealing livestock from farms; and physical threats against hacendados (Inteview: Gustavo Vallejo April 1, 1998).

International human rights organizations, such as Amnesty International, intervened in this situation in Yuracruz because over 14 deaths of indigenous people and rapes (to women who were 77 and 91 years of age) had been reported due to the violent tactics of the security forces. Security forces were reported to be utilizing guns to control crowds, as well as physically handling people to move them. Ecuadorian newspapers do not report this physical abuse, or the rapes. However, the government of Ecuador did intervene in the situation in response to the international outcry. In December 1992, Durán negotiated with CONAIE for the financial support for the indigenous groups to regain their land (Selverston 1994: 147).

THE 1993–1994 UPRISINGS

The Durán administration in 1993–1994 attempted to implement liberal economic policies with the intent of modernizing Ecuador, such as an Agrarian Reform Law and a Modernization Law, as well as various privatization and exploration policies for oil industries. All of these initiatives were met with protest, at times violent, by indigenous groups, organized by CONAIE. The government response to the indigenous mobilization was often violent and lacked negotiation unless met by international pressures.

One example of conflictive interaction is between indigenous peoples in the Amazon and the military. The military, under government order, is utilized to aid and protect oil company blocks in this region. As the government is owner of all subsoil rights, the military is legitimated in its protection of these blocks of land. However, the protection of these blocks includes land on which indigenous communities have lived for centuries. Due to the conflict between oil companies and indigenous communities over land usage and rights issues, there are occasional to frequent (depending upon the block) demonstrations at seismic testing sites or protests. This contentious activity ranges from peaceful demonstrations to kidnappings of oil company employees. The military has assumed the responsibility of protecting oil company employees and equipment, thus placing themselves in a situation of conflict with the indigenous communities. Organizations, such as OPIP (in Pastaza) and FOIN (in Napo) have reported incidents of coercive or forceful behavior on the part of the military toward indigenous communities. These actions have been met with strong criticism by international activist organizations (Selverston 1994: 148). Since this criticism and increased transnational mobilization, including negotiations with oil company and government representatives, forceful military intervention has declined.

Furthermore, the national government has initiated various modernization plans, hailed by the United States, the IMF and the World Bank, which have prompted demonstrations and protests not only joined by indigenous groups, but also labor unions, teachers, and students. On May 26, 1994, Indians, students, and labor unions protested the new economic modernization plans. This created a work stoppage that had not occurred in Ecuador in over 14 years. Moreover, the indigenous groups had now mobilized beyond their own communities to incorporate other groups that were affected by the new plans.

On June 13, 1994, President Durán signed a New Agrarian Reform Law into effect. This law was intended to create a free market for farm produce, strengthen individual titles to land, provide investment funds to small farmers, and to abolish the land reform agency (IERAC). For indigenous groups, this law is controversial because it allows communally held plots of land to be divided and sold, or mortgaged. Fifty-eight percent of Ecuador's rural land belongs to peasant communities, primarily indigenous, and 41 per cent is privately or state owned. It is this 58 per cent that is jeopardized (*Inter Press Service* June 3, 1993). President Luis Macas of CONAIE argues that the "breakup of communal lands will mean the dissolution of indigenous communities by destroying their geographical and political integrity" (Van Cott 1994, *The Journal of Commerce*).

On June 14, 1994, protests ensued in response to the signing of the Agrarian Reform Law. While organized by CONAIE, the FUT (Ecuador's largest labor union), students, teachers, and the Catholic Church supported the protests. CONAIE organized the blocking by 56 communities of access roads to oil drilling sites. Fifteen of the 21 major arteries of transportation were closed, causing food and oil shortages. In the town of Canar, looting and vandalism occurred. By June 23, one hundred Indians had occupied the Riobamba Cathedral, in Chimborazo, supported by a local bishop. Reports of Indian deaths numbered from two to four or more. However, by mid-July, the government and CONAIE, aided by negotiations with the Church and non-governmental organizations, reached an agreement to reform the land law (Van Cott 1994; Van Cott 1993; *Latin American Regional Reports 1994*: 3; *Latin American Weekly Report 1994*: 290; Long 1993: 1).

Another instance of complex interaction between the indigenous groups, the national government, and the international system is the protests throughout 1994 against oil companies. The Amazon, due to its international ecological value and the development of oil and other mineral extraction processes, has become a focus for the indigenous movement of South America. Amazonian Indian groups have sought for many years to expel foreign oil companies and Petroecuador from their land. However, recently, these companies have been negotiating directly with the indigenous groups in response to protests. One such incident that has alerted oil companies to the demands of indigenous groups is an Ecuadorian case currently waiting trial in the New York Federal District Court. It is a $1 billion federal class action suit filed against Texaco, a U.S. based multinational oil corporation, on behalf of the Cofán, Secoya, and other Indians in the Amazon region. The Indians charge that Texaco has contaminated the rainforest environment with crude oil wastes, increasing the risk of cancer for their community members. The attorney for the Indians, Joseph Kohn, of Philadelphia, charges that Texaco dumped over 3,000 gallons of crude oil per day along the dirt roads of the rainforest (Van Cott 1994: 11; *United Press International* November 2, 1991).

The Amazonian Indians have organized on an international level with regard to the oil issue. Indigenous communities in Peru have also filed suit against Texaco for their affected areas. Each indigenous community impacted by the oil drilling and the environment has filed a suit against Texaco. These suits will be tried in the U.S. court system, attracting media attention, and the Indians are represented by U.S. law firms and supported by various non-governmental organizations and transnational organizations. Through international media attention, the Indians have lobbied the Ecuadorian government to postpone its international oil field auction in order to create an environmental management plan and a special sustainable development fund. This auction would give international oil companies access to over 8 million acres of indigenous community territory for the exploration and extraction of petroleum. OPIP (Pastaza Indians) would be the most harshly affected by losing over 600,000 hectares of their territory, which was to be awarded to them by the government (*Inter Press Service* December 14, 1993).

Various international and transnational organizations have aided in the indigenous communities' cause to save their territories in the Amazon. Groups such as the Action for the Defense of the Tropical Forest from the U.S., The Future is in Our Hands from Norway, and Friends of the Earth from Britain have promoted boycott campaigns against Texaco and any other oil companies which drill in Ecuador. The U.S. non-governmental organization, Center for Economic and Social Rights, has studied the Amazonian region and supports the indigenous efforts. The Independent Commission on International Humanitarian Issues and Amnesty International have also supported Indian environmental and human rights concerns, in addition to developing and implementing international media campaigns about the environmental abuses in the Ecuadorian Amazon. Furthermore, some environmental groups are criticizing the World Bank for its new Global Environmental Facility (GEF) grant to protect Ecuador's forest. Some environmental groups claim this is a form of "greenwashing" the issue to allow for modernization and privatization programs that harm the Indians and their environment (*InterPress Service* May 20, 1994; Jones 1994: 10; *Inter Press Service* March 30, 1994). Finally, Indian communities are soliciting international funds to persuade the government to agree to a debt-for-land swap. Therefore, the indigenous communities of the Amazon have utilized international organizations and resources to voice their concerns on a wide array of levels from local to global.

As David Holmstrom argues, "Today, more than ever, Indians are less likely to be seen as powerless and inferior in Latin America. They are demanding rights and constitutional status, both conditions long denied by the ruling classes" (1993: 9). These demands are being made not only to national and international systems, but also directly to multinational oil companies, which have also negotiated with the Indians. For instance, companies like Maxus are building classrooms, paying for bilingual materials, and giving scholarships to the indigenous communities. However, CONAIE leaders argue that this is not sufficient. These groups demand environmental clean up, legal rights to their land, and autonomous territories. One new plan calls for oil companies to share 1 percent of their profits with indigenous communities. The transnational advocacy networks of the Amazon in this case are very different from the Sierra case, which has far fewer resources and less international exposure.

ECUADOR: PRESENT AND FUTURE

After the 1994 protest, indigenous mobilization took a new course. In 1996, Pachakutik, a new political party representing indigenous concerns, was founded. This party ran candidates in presidential and congressional elections. While it was not successful in obtaining the presidency (although it was in third place), it did win two national Congressional seats from the provinces of Loja and Imbabura. Both representatives were Quichua Indians from the Sierra. This was the beginning of change for the indigenous movement.

In February 1997, the newly elected president, Abdala Bucaram, was ousted from office and replaced, after some constitutional confusion and debate, with the president of the National Congress, Fabian Alarcon. During the Bucaram presidency (August 1996 through February 5, 1997), a Ministry of Ethnic Affairs was created and Shuar leader Raphael Pandam was appointed its first Minister. However, the Ministry and his title were eliminated after the overthrow of the Bucaram administration. While the Ministry no longer exists as a form of indigenous representation, the indigenous movement was very active in coordinating with other social movements during the organization of the weeklong demonstrations against former-President Bucaram.

Interim-President Alarcón and his administration held a referendum vote in April 1997 on whether to call for a Constitutional Assembly. The reform process was overwhelmingly supported. The Assembly included various Amazonian and Sierra indigenous leaders. One of the primary leaders from the Sierra was Nina Pacari, an Otavalan Quicha, and from the Amazon, Marcelo Chumbi, a Shuar. However, the Constituent Assembly failed to devise a new constitution in the allotted time. The president of the Assembly, Oswaldo Hurtado, resigned from his position and the Assembly was finally disbanded due to its inability to come to a consensus on constitutional reformation. More recently, the CONAIE and indigenous leaders participated in the protests of January 2000 against then-President Jamil Mahuad and have led a coalition in the National Congress for constitutional reform, calling for a multi-ethnic state.

The indigenous movement of Ecuador has made, over the years, some significant progress in obtaining its goals. Where once indigenous peoples could not even vote in national elections, they now are competing in presidential elections and are represented in the national Congress. Furthermore, the indigenous movement of Ecuador has become an active member of civil society, sometimes coordinating with other domestic social movements, as was the case in the ousting of former-President Bucaram in February 1997. However, a great difference still exists between Amazonian and Sierra indigenous organizations. The office of ECUARUNARI (The Sierra regional organization) is in a very poor section of Quito with no infrastructure. The office of CONFENIAE, the Amazonian regional organization, is located next to the National Congress building with two fax machines, various computers with Internet connections, walkie talkies to communicate with leaders in the Congress, and four secretaries. Although the Sierra indigenous peoples have always been much more involved in the national political system and, in general, have had more resources, than Amazonian indigenous organizations, Amazonian Indians have managed to overcome these obstacles and re-organize on a transnational level. For this reason, the distinct Amazonian case will be the focus of this research project.

CONCLUSION

Knowledge of the historical precursors to transnational social movements and advocacy networks can shed light on the intricacies of the networks and the reasons for their effectiveness. The historical background of the transnational indigenous rights movement elucidates the process of transnational network formation and the development of transnational frames and strategies of mobilization. This process, in combination with the more specific case study of Ecuador, highlights the reasons why particular movement organizations opt to join transnational networks, and as will be seen in the following chapters, and the reasons they are generally more successful.

A common element among all actors in the transnational indigenous movement is the lack of representation within their own countries and the need to seek resources outside of the state realm. Amazonian indigenous groups joined these advocacy networks beginning in the mid-1980s through transnational networks of environmentalists, academics, and

NGO representatives.. Thus, Amazonian groups coordinate their policies on a transnational level among specific indigenous groups, COICA, the transnational social movement organization, and the numerous transnational non-governmental organizations in the United Nations.

The historical underpinnings of the transnational indigenous rights movement, focusing on the Amazon and Ecuador, demonstrate the significance of including transnational factors in the analysis of social movements. In addition, this chapter illustrates the importance of the inclusion of domestic factors in the analysis of transnational actors. As the state and its functions evolve in a changing global system in which private, non-state actors obtain increasing authority, the inclusion of societal and transnational variables in international relations theory will be necessary. Moreover, a study of modern transnational social movement organizations and advocacy networks cannot evade the antecedents to these complex processes.

NOTES

[1] For more information on historical precursors, also see Sikkink, Kathryn and Margaret Keck (1998). *Activists Beyond Borders*. Ithaca: Cornell University Press, Chapter 2.

[2] See Julian Burger (1987). *Report from the Frontier: The State of the World's Indigenous Peoples*. London: Zed Books,Ltd.; Bice Maiguashca (1996). "The Role of Ideas in a Changing World Order: The International Indigenous Movement, 1975–1990." *Centre for Research on Latin America and the Caribbean Occasional Papers*, Number 4:Ontario: York University.

[3] The following is a list of the eight organizations with consultative status: The World Council of Churches, The International Indian Treaty Council, The Indian Law Resource Center, the Inuit Circumpolar Conference, the Indian World Association, the Four Directions Council, the National Aborigine and Islander Service Secretariat, the National Indian Youth Council, and the Grand Council of Crees (as a non-governmental ethnic group, not an organization).

[4] For another detailed explanation of the formation of transnational indigenous networks, see Franke Wilmer (1993). *The Indigenous Voice in World Politics*. Newbury Park: Sage Publications.

[5] Some Ecuadorian Indians boycotted the most recent census survey, making population percentages difficult to estimate.

[6] The term "uprising" is the literal translation of the word "levantamiento" in Spanish. Ecuadorian scholars and news sources refer to indigenous demonstrations and protests as such.

[7] See also, Ramon, Galo,ed. (1992). *Actores de una Decada Gananda: Tribus, Comunidades y Campesinos en la Modernidad*. Quito: Comunidec.

[8]Deprivation refers to the theory of relative deprivation which contends that "people's discontent about unjust deprivation is the primary motivation for political action," See Ted R. Gurr (1993). *Minorities At Risk*. Washington,D.C.: United States Institute of Peace. This research project employs a combination of relative deprivation theory, group mobilization theory, and transnational relations theory.
[9]Indigenous peoples did contribute to the development of local and regional political systems in the areas outside of Quito, the capital. However, their presence on a national level is not witnessed until the 1990s.

CHAPTER FOUR
Transnational Advocacy Networks in the Ecuadorian Amazon

INTRODUCTION

LTHOUGH THE AMAZONIAN POPULATION OF ECUADOR IS ONE OF THE smallest indigenous populations in all of Latin America and one of the most resource-poor, its representatives have managed to organize outside of state boundaries to confront petroleum development in their region, including direct negotiations with oil companies, seeking land grants, and obtaining international funding. How do such resource-poor groups confront a situation in which national government institutions are non-responsive and international market actors have entered their region for development? An option which is not so new, but increasingly more popular, is to organize and mobilize transnationally. These once resource-poor actors have created venues of communication, funding, and organization through a process of transnational networks and transnational social movement organizations to overcome their national/domestic situation and to open new political opportunities on both domestic and transnational levels.

This chapter will demonstrate, through an historical analysis of the development of transnational contentious collective action in the Ecuadorian Amazon, that transnational networks change the collective action strategies of the domestic social movement organization, such that the strategies incorporate ideas, discourse, frames, and tactics that derive from the transnational level. In the case of transnational contentious collective action in the Ecuadorian Amazon, transnational networks have changed the originally aggressive and reactive collective action strategies (i.e., violent protests, take-overs or destruction of oil drilling sites, violence toward *colonos-* those who work for the oil companies) to pro-active, more peaceful strategies, focused on negotiation and professionalism.

Moreover, the formation and evolution of transnational networks, which in many cases circumvent the state level, have given non-state actors on societal and transnational levels an authority[1] on national and international levels that they did not have previously. In the case of the Ecuadorian Amazon, indigenous confederations, multinational oil companies, and international and national non-governmental organizations negotiate and share information in a transnational network which in many cases does not include the participation of state actors or, in others, in which the state plays a very weak role. Thus, this project illustrates the authority of non-state actors in an international system with multiple levels of analysis.

The case of the Ecuadorian Amazon has parallels with other cases of transnational contentious collective action, particularly in an international system in which transnational market actors interact with resource-poor countries which do not provide responsive institutions to social movement organizations. The model utilized for this case may be applied to other cases within Latin America, such as Peru, which shares many Amazonian transnational networks with Ecuador, Colombia, Mexico, and Venezuela, or in many South East Asian countries in which multinational timber corporations are negotiating with local populations in tropical rainforest areas. As market actors and other non-state international actors increase their number and activity in the international system, transnational contentious collective action will become a common form of social movement mobilization. For this reason, it is important to understand the dynamics of this transnational process and its outcomes.

ASSUMPTIONS

Most of what we know about social movements is based in the nation-state and the domestic political system. However, social movements are not necessarily constrained by the state and in fact, mobilize across borders with other non-state actors. Recent examples of the transnationalization of social movements have been human rights, environmental, women's, and indigenous peoples movements.[2] Each of these movements utilizes resources from transnational actors, draws upon support from transnational organizations (intergovernmental and non-governmental), and acts to change policies and/or enter the political process of both the state and transnational organizations (such as the United Nations and the Organization of American States).

In addition to the increase of scholarship on the transnationalization of social movements, new theories of globalization, global civil society, and the decline of the state have been formulated.[3] While states have not ceased to exist and the international system still functions via state institutions, leaders, and law, much of the social movement literature does not take account of the dynamics of a global system in which multiple levels of political opportunities, resources, mobilization, and policy outcomes exist.

This is not a new phenomenon in the international system. A world economy has existed for centuries and communication and diffusion of ideas among and between cultures and peoples have been well documented. However, the recent increase (since the 1960s) in non-state actors, coupled with the rapidity of communication and international travel,[4] have directly impacted not only state to state, or international institution to state relations, but they have directly altered the form of social movements (on a sub-national level), imparting upon them a transnational frame. Likewise, these sub-national social movement organizations (SMOs) have transcended their national setting and have enmeshed their identities and ideas within the global arena.

This chapter, and the larger project, seeks to re-shape these "conceptual boundaries" in such a way that scholars of domestic politics and scholars of international politics can see reflections in the political activities of actors above and below the level of the state, and their interactions. I assume that the international system is not solely a dichotomy between international anarchy and state sovereignty, but rather includes a plethora of actors with varying levels of authority, which includes, but is not exclusive to, states. The assumption of authority of non-state actors in the international system (including actors of the societal level) provides the basis to analyze impacts and outcomes of transnational contentious politics on various levels from local to societal to international.

FRAMEWORK FOR ANALYSIS

To better understand the divisions between transnational social networks and transnational social movements, this chapter will focus on and analyze transnational issue networks. However, within the transnational environment of the Ecuadorian Amazon, indigenous confederations utilize both forms of collective action (transnational issue networks and transnational social movements) to achieve their goals. Therefore, in order to illustrate the intricacies of both forms of transnational contentious collective action, this chapter will focus on issue networks and Chapter Five will focus on transnational social movements, while simultaneously including the links between both forms of transnational contentious collective action.

As Sidney Tarrow argues, transnational issue networks differ from transnational social movements in that transnational issue networks involve "issue-oriented" action, while transnational social movements involve "interpersonal social networks" (Tarrow 1996:24). Thus, transnational issue networks may be sustained, but they are not integrated in the domestic social network of the social movement. While the larger project surrounding this chapter does analyze both forms of transnational contentious collective action, this chapter will focus more on transnational networks and how they influence collective action strategies.

THE ECUADORIAN AMAZON AND INDIGENOUS PEOPLES

The Ecuadorian Amazon occupies half of the geographic area of the entire country, or about 131,000 square kilometers. Although the region is geographically large, the population of the region only accounts for 3.9 percent of the total population (indigenous and non-indigenous combined) of the country, which in turn is divided into five Amazonian provinces (Sucumbíos, Napo, Pastaza, Morona Santiago, and Zamora Chinchipe).[5] This region has always been less integrated into the national system, politically, culturally, and economically than the Coastal and Highland regions. While multinational development in the Highland began hundreds of years ago, the Amazon has just recently experienced development, starting in 1923, but not on a large scale until the entry of Texaco in 1972.

Indigenous peoples comprise about 40 percent of the Ecuadorian population, or 4,728,000 people (Psacharopoulos and Patrinos 1994: 28). Indigenous peoples of the Amazon encompass 2.5 percent of the total indigenous population (1.0 percent of the total population), or about 120,000 people (Pandor 1990, applying UN Population Estimates 1995).[6] The Shuar and the Quichua, numbering over 100,000, are the two largest groups in the region. The other groups are the Achuar (2,500), the Siona-Secoya (600), the Cofán (460), the Huaorani (600), and other small indigenous groups (CONAIE 1989:35–37)[7]. Despite their small percentage of the total indigenous population, Amazonian peoples are leaders of the indigenous rights movement and maintain the closest level of contact with private, transnational actors.

However, contact with transnational actors began before the post-1972 development of oil in the region. In the 1940s, with the activity of Shell Oil Company, the Summer Linguistic Institute/Wycliffe Bible Translator Inc. (SLI/WBT) sent Protestant missionaries to the region to convert the indigenous populations. In 1964, the first Indian federation formed through the aid of Salesian missionaries, called the Federation of the Shuar Centers. This group of Ecuadorian Indians established programs for their communities outside of state programs. These programs included bilingual education, health care, and improved technologies for cattle ranching. This organization was founded to strengthen indigenous organization and communities in response to the new influence of oil companies and employees in the Amazon. In the late 1980s, the SLI/WBT left the Ecuadorian Amazon, but missionary work still continues through other religious groups, both Protestant and Catholic.[8] Currently in the Amazon, the indigenous confederations are organized, funded, and mobilize separately from religious organizations. Thus, indigenous transnational organization from this region began with the penetration and influence of transnational actors—those including missionaries, oil companies, and oil company employees.

Following the Shuar Federation, the Federation of the Indigenous Organization of Napo (FOIN) formed in 1973 with other Quichua confederations in the Northern region (see table below), and later the Organization for Indigenous Peoples of Pastaza (OPIP), which together represent over 60 Quichua communities. There are provincial indigenous organizations throughout the Amazonian region. They combine the indigenous traditions of shamanism with more western forms of organization, such as a president, a vice-president, and a secretary. These groups were primarily concerned with struggles for land. They have currently assumed leadership positions within the national organization of indigenous peoples, and have expanded their interests to include the environment, human rights, education, health care, and increased political participation on a national level.

In 1980, the groups of the Amazon joined together to form the Confederation of Indigenous Nationalities of the Ecuadorian Amazon (CONFENIAE). This regional organization has members of the Shuar and Quichua peoples in leadership positions, in addition to representations of the Achuar, Huaorani, Cofán, Siona, and Secoya tribes. Through this alliance, the organization has brought their issues to public attention and to the political agendas of national and international groups. They also have formed alliances with environmental and human rights organizations, in addition to bringing "oil companies and the government to the negotiating table, particularly regarding development practices in the Amazon" (Selverston 1994: 136). Most importantly, the regional association has sought to protect and extend land rights, and continues to do so.

The national indigenous organization of Ecuador is CONAIE. It was first formed by the union of ECUARUNARI (the Sierra indigenous council) and CONFENIAE in 1980 and originally called the Coordinating Council of Indigenous Nationalities of Ecuador (CONACNIE). Following this union, the coastal Indian communities formed a regional group,

COICE (Coordinator of Indigenous Organizations of the Coast of Ecuador), and it joined the two former groups to form the contemporary CONAIE. Amazonian peoples participate in the CONAIE, and are currently in executive positions (specifically members of OPIP), which has helped the Amazonians in negotiations with the government and oil companies (Selverston 1994: 135–136).

Indian Organizations of the Ecuadorian Amazon

Organization	Ethnic Group	Year	Province
Shuar Federation	Shuar & Achuar	1962	Morona, Zamora
AIPSE	Shuar & Achuar	1963	Morona
FOIN	Quichua	1969	Napo
FCUNAE	Quichua	1976	Napo
OPIP	Quichua	1979	Pastaza
FOISE	Quichua	1980	Sucumbíos
CONFENIAE	multi-ethnic region	1980	Amazon
OISSE[9]	Siona-Secoya	1986	Sucumbíos
COFÁN	Cofán	1990	Sucumbíos
ONHAE	Huaorani	1990	Napo

Source: Fernando Serrano 1993:pp.4.

The level of organization since the late-1980s has expanded to a transnational level in this region. Currently, there are over 200 NGOs (national and transnational) working in the Ecuadorian Amazon for the preservation of the environment and sustainable development. As Ortiz and Varea note, these new methods of information and communication from national and transnational levels have created the "green panorama" in the region, "as an expression of the cultural hegemony of new capitalism and its ideology of safe management of global resources prompted by many western conservationists" (Ortiz and Varea 1995:36).

In fact, the level of organization in the region has evolved from transnational networks between NGOs, MNCs, and SMOs to transnational social movements, in which there are various confederations of indigenous peoples from the Amazon Basin in different countries working together, sharing information, and coordinating strategies. One group, formed in 1992, called COICA (Coordinator of Indigenous Confederations of the Amazon Basin) and a second called The Coalition for Amazonian Peoples and their Environment, formed in 1993, work in conjunction on common issues of the Amazons. COICA focuses within the respective countries, while the Coalition works on an international level, being based in Washington, D.C., to coordinate funding and lobbying of international organizations. The members of these TSMOs meet periodically during the year to organize efforts and to "touch base" with regional and local concerns. The members of the indigenous confederations within this study are all active members of COICA and the Coalition. [10]

OVERVIEW OF THE CASES

The following cases provide a comparative-historical analysis of the development and evolution of transnational networks and transnational social movements in the Ecuadorian Amazon. Three phases will be analyzed: (1) the initiation of oil development and relations with indigenous populations (or, the Texaco phase beginning in 1972); (2) the increase in transnational networks and negotiations and the formation of indigenous confederations (or, the ARCO phase from 1988—late 1990s); (3) the professionalization and transnationalization of the indigenous confederations and increase in negotiations with oil companies (or, the Oxy phase from 1996–1999). I have chosen to highlight representative confederations and oil companies.

Phase I: Texaco (1972–1993)

Oil exploration in the Ecuadorian Amazon began in 1909, bringing international capital to the Ecuadorian government. In 1923, the Leonard Exploration Company obtained land in the North (Sumaco) and in the South (Macas) of the Amazon to explore for petroleum deposits. These activities concluded in 1931. Then, in 1937, the Anglo Saxum Petroleum Company obtained concessions of land for exploration, but was unsuccessful. In 1939, the Shell Company Ecuador also unsuccessfully searched for petroleum deposits. The Shell Co. was the first company to bring missionaries to the Amazon to convert the indigenous populations. All of the above accords for oil exploration were conducted between the Ecuadorian state and the oil company itself. Although indigenous populations were living in the areas of exploration, no communities were consulted.

Then, in 1967 Texaco-Gulf Consortium gained positive results from exploration tests. These positive results prompted large-scale exploration for petroleum in the Ecuadorian Amazon. From 1972 until 1982, the Consortium Texaco-Gulf produced and exported oil under the Hydrocarbon Law of 1972. The law created the Ecuadorian State Petroleum Corporation (CEPE); demanded that CEPE receive 25 percent of all rights and profits of the Consortium Texaco-Gulf; and stipulated that CEPE acquire 62.4 percent of the shares of the Consortium (Fundación Natura 1996:11–13).

In August 1972, oil production began and a 313–mile trans-Andean production pipeline was built from Lago Agrio (in the Northern Amazon) across 12,000–foot mountains and down to the Pacific Ocean. Production of petroleum quadrupled from 1972 to 1977, increasing Ecuador's GNP from $2.2 billion in 1971 to $5.9 billion in 1977. Petroleum revenues were utilized for education, rural loans, and infrastructural development. The petroleum industry became a significant actor within Ecuadorian economic and political policymaking.

The Texaco-Gulf Consortium was closely involved in governmental policymaking during the period of military government of Ecuador, which ended with the democratic transition in 1979. For example, General Jarrín, Minister of Natural Resources, was sharply criticized for his inefficient management of CEPE. So, in September 1974, Texaco-Gulf promoted his removal from office, including a private press campaign supporting his ousting. Again in 1976, Texaco-Gulf initiated a campaign against nationalistic oil policies. Thus, Texaco, although a transnational actor, established an authoritative role within the Ecuadorian national political system (Martz 1987:133–154).

After transition to democracy in 1979, Ecuador increased oil exploration in the Amazon and Texaco re-invested in oil development in the region. Until 1984 the Texaco-Gulf Consortium was the primary producer and developer of oil in the Amazon. However, between 1984 and 1993 the country had six rounds of international licensing for oil development, which added twelve more oil companies to the Amazonian region (Fundación Natura 1996:12–13).

Until 1992, when Texaco closed its Ecuadorian accounts, it continued to produce and export oil in conjunction with Petroecuador (changed from CEPE in 1990) without intervention by social actors, such as NGOs and indigenous confederations. In addition, no environmental policy was established by the Ecuadorian government until 1984 with the foundation of the Dirección General de Medio Ambiente (DIGEMA) under the Ministry of Energy and Mines. It was also not until the early 1990s that the government required yearly environmental impact reports to be filed. Thus, Texaco had acquired a private, authoritative role within the Ecuadorian government and society with few controls.

Phase I: Part II (The Initiation of Transnational Networks)

However, in 1993 it was discovered that the lack of controls over oil development by Texaco had left irreparable damages, social and environmental, in the Ecuadorian Amazon. Until this time, no one had protested nor organized against Texaco, nor had there been negotiations with anyone other than state actors. The environmental damage from 15 petroleum camps and 22 stations of production in Napo and Sucumbíos has been estimated to be greater than that of the Exxon-Valdez spill, and covers over 20 years of petroleum extraction (El Comercio May 13, 1997:C12).

In 1993, the indigenous group of Cofánes in the Amazon initiated a lawsuit against Texaco Oil Company in the United States. Although the Cofánes are a small group and have fewer resources than others in the Amazon, they have utilized new, transnational strategies to change oil policy in their region. For instance, they have established an eco-tourism business in the Amazon through funding from international NGOs such as RAN.

The Cofán indigenous peoples number from 460 to 1200 peoples, depending upon various estimates. Their formal organization did not develop until 1990, in response to the environmental harm to their lands by Texaco. The Cofán are represented in and act jointly with CONFENI-AE. Prior to 1993, the Cofán had a strong identity, but low levels of mobilization and resources. However, since 1990, the Cofán have successfully mobilized and have gained transnational resources from U.S. law firms.

In November 1993, the Cofán filed a class-action suit in New York Federal Court against Texaco, seeking $1.5 billion in damages to be invested in a clean up project. Cristóbal Bonifaz, an Ecuadorian and lawyer for the law firm Khon, Nast, and Graf in Philadelphia, has donated his time, and firm time and resources, to their case. Judith Kimerling, an environmental attorney for the Natural Resources Defense Council (NRDC) and author of *Amazon Crude*, has also joined the suit, in support of the Cofán. On the national level, NGOs with international funding such as Acción Ecológica, Fundación Natura, and la Campaña Amazonía por la Vida and international NGOs such as Rainforest Action Network (RAN), National Wildlife Federation (NWF), and NRDC have supported the Cofánes in a transnational network of information and mobilization.

The class action suit in 1993 began a new period of transnationalization in the Ecuadorian Amazon for the indigenous populations. In 1994, an international boycott of Texaco Oil Company was initiated in the United States and Amazonian South American Countries, organized by the Cofánes, Acción Ecológica, Fundación Natura, the Coalition for Amazonian Peoples and the Environment, and COICA. On May 2, 1996, The Coalition for Amazonian Peoples and their Environment funded a trip for sixty indigenous delegates to the Ecuadorian National Congress to protest an agreement signed between the government and Texaco for the reparation of the environmental damage to the Amazon. The Coalition, COICA, Acción Ecológica, Fundación Natura, and CONFENIAE have all circulated newsletters, e-mail messages, and Internet articles about the Texaco situation and the Cofánes in Ecuador as part of the transnational network of discourse and mobilization.

This law suit challenges the national sovereignty of the Ecuadorian state. The Ecuadorian government has intervened on the side of Texaco, claiming that this lawsuit affronts its national sovereignty. Later, on November 25, 1996, the Attorney General, Leonides Plaza, announced that the government was considering intervention on the plaintiff's behalf. The intervention of the state in this case suggests two observations. First, the Ecuadorian state has lost some of its sovereignty to private actors. Second, the corporate power of Texaco is so important that the state intervened on its behalf. The state, at the same time, pressured by international environmental concerns, issued a statement against ecological degradation by petroleum extraction on behalf of the plaintiffs (Amazon Update December 15, 1996:1). This case and issue-area demonstrate the complex, multi-faceted role of the state.

However, Judge Vincent Broderick ruled that he will hear the case in New York if Texaco's decisions in the Cofán area were made in its New York offices. Since that time, Texaco has begun implementation of a clean up program and has attempted to settle out of court with the Cofánes. In the summer 1995, 25,000 Peruvians also filed suit against Texaco for similar damages (Jochnik 1995:5). Thus far, all proposals have been rejected. The case is still pending (Switkes 1994) and as of mid-2001, the Texaco clean up plan was approved and had begun its initial stages in the Northern regions of the Amazon.

Since this lawsuit, the Cofán have been consulted directly by oil companies about their land in the Cuyabeño Reserve. The state oil company, Petro Ecuador, and the Cofánes have signed an agreement stating that Pedro Ecuador has to ask written permission and receive approval before entering the reserve. The Cofánes also must be included in the supervision of oil drilling sites and may form monitoring committees for protection against environmental degradation. Although the Cofán are a small group, their protests have escalated since the inception of the 1993 law suit. For instance, in November 1993, members of the Cofán community forced workers off a Petro Ecuador drilling site within the Cuyabeño Reserve (Colitt November 22, 1993:7). Since making direct contact with MNCs, they have changed their mobilization strategies to include "western-style" organization, using newsletters, e-mail messages, and Internet articles about their progress and continuing direct negotiations with oil MNCs.

Phase II: ARCO (1988–1999)

Arco Oriente Inc. began seismic testing in Block 10 of the Amazon in 1988. Arco was one of the twelve oil companies that received licensing privileges after 1984. It is also one of six companies in the Amazon currently which has passed the exploration phase and is now in development and production phase (Fundación Natura 1996:13). ARCO and its relations with the indigenous confederation of Pastaza (OPIP) are analyzed to illustrate the transitional phase of transnational networks within this region; they have developed complex strategies and techniques of information exchange which were learned from the previous Texaco phase. In 1994, Victor Villamil, president of OPIP, commented that his province of Pastaza did not want to "confront the social problems ... which had occurred with the petroleum company Texaco in Napo and Sucumbíos" (Fernández 1994:D8). Thus, transnational contentious collective action in the Amazon has been a process of learning from previous experiences.

The Organization of Indigenous Peoples of Pastaza (OPIP) was founded in 1977 in response to the colonization of their lands by oil companies and oil company employees since the early-1960s. In an interview with the indigenous leader and technical advisor of OPIP, Leonardo Viteri, he commented that his organization learned from the events in the Northern Amazon with Texaco. He stated, "There were no paths within the country for indigenous peoples in the Amazon, except Petro Ecuador, which basically did not exist for indigenous confederations. So, it was easier to look for resources outside of the country" (Interview March 6, 1997). Viteri noted the example of a project that OPIP had had with the state that OPIP since 1980, in which they had never seen state officials nor plans to initiate the project.

OPIP is one of the most highly organized and mobilized indigenous organizations in the Amazon. They have many more transnational networks and resources than the Cofánes, and have maintained a "pro-active" position with the oil company ARCO. The SMO itself has three programs:

(1) ethnic group development, (2) inter-community relations, and (3) literacy and educational programs. Like many other groups in the Amazon, OPIP began its transnational contacts with missionaries. However, OPIP, since that time, has developed highly complex transnational networks without religious affiliations. Viteri commented that among the most important features of OPIP, aside from its own inter-group relations, are its transnational relations. OPIP in 1990 opened two representations in Europe, one in Spain and one in Belgium. In 1997, they planned to open an office in San Francisco, California and in 1998, an office in Asia. These offices are formal representations with an OPIP representative and an INGO sponsor working in them and relaying vital information to the main OPIP office and other INGOs. Viteri himself had traveled many times to their offices in Europe and initiated the California office due to his connections with Rainforest Action Network (RAN) and his former studies at the University of California, Berkeley.[11]

OPIP also maintains many active transnational connections with INGOs. They currently are working on projects with RAN and the Coalition for Amazonian Peoples and their Environment. Also the European Union is financing environmental projects in Pastaza via a $2 million grant managed by IBIS-Denmark. IBIS works directly with OPIP in Puyo, Pastaza on programs such as education, agriculture, health, and transportation. They also provide technical and legal advising during negotiations with oil companies and are training OPIP members in petroleum technology so they can better advise their populations. IBIS is also one of the supporters of the Amazanga Institute, which was founded in 1992, for the purposes of scientific research and technical consultation on the environment. Leonardo Viteri, OPIP technical consultant, is also the president of the Amazanga Institute. IBIS coordinates its funding and programs with other INGOs that work with OPIP, such as Oxfam America and the Inter-American Foundation. These three INGOs also coordinate programs between CONFENIAE (the Amazonian regional indigenous confederation) and OPIP. Thus, these INGOs not only strengthen communication and networks transnationally and within OPIP, but they work to strengthen the regional, inter-community Amazonian networks.[12]

Furthermore, Arco Oriente Inc. is an actor within this transnational network. OPIP negotiates and communicates directly with ARCO officials. Arco officials also communicate and share information with INGOs, such as Fundación Natura (sponsored by World Wildlife Fund, WWF), Fundación Antisana (sponsored by the Nature Conservancy), and Conservation International. These INGOs have consulted with Arco about environmental standards and cleanup.[13] Sixto Méndez, former Manager of

Environment, Health, and Safety for ARCO admitted that ARCO did not have good relations with all INGOs, but were nonetheless open to communication. INGOs differ in motivations and goals. Thus, their activity and relationships with various actors differ as well. In this case, there were INGOs that worked in conjunction with ARCO and there were INGOs that would not communicate with ARCO. While Fundación Natura and Fundación Antisana communicate with OPIP and ARCO to create appropriate development plans for both actors, Acción Ecológica and RAN preferred to work solely with the indigenous populations to prevent oil production.

The history of communication between ARCO and OPIP began in April 1989 when the Sarayacu Association of Pastaza paralyzed seismic activity in the area through a community-wide demonstration in front of the sites. The community claims that they were not consulted on the activity in this area and considered these areas sacred to Quichua culture. In May 1989, there were 10 days of discussion between government officials, ARCO and Petro Ecuador representatives, and indigenous organizations (CONFENIAE, CONAIE, FCUNAE, and FOIN), led by OPIP. The discussions took place in Sarayacu, an OPIP stronghold and one of the most politically active Quichua communities. OPIP blocked the air strip until an agreement was reached. The agreement was called the "Sarayacu Accords" and called for the cessation of oil exploration in the OPIP lands until they received compensation from oil companies for environmental damage. It included a promise from the state to stop further exploration of natural resources that would harm the environment. The Sarayacu Accords were the first step in negotiations between the state, indigenous peoples, and oil companies. OPIP had a major role in these meetings. It utilized the private power of ARCO and its relationships with the state to strengthen OPIP's role as a political actor. Moreover, OPIP was aided through the resources of international and national NGOs, such as RAN.

The stature gained in the Sarayacu Accords helped OPIP increase its mobilization. For instance, in 1990 the Borja administration began a sixth round of oil exploration rights in block 10, the OPIP land. In response to this, OPIP organized a hunger strike by 82 people in the Santo Domingo Church in Quito, with CONFENIAE and CONAIE. The government surrounded the church, but by June 2, indigenous peoples in the Sierra, Napo, and Pastaza mobilized, blocked roads, and marched in the streets. On June 6, the Borja administration negotiated a settlement with CONAIE. By August 22, 1990, the Borja administration met with 120 indigenous leaders, including Leonardo Viteri, director of the Amazanga Institute, representing OPIP. The OPIP document demanded control over natural resources, including subsoil, but was rejected by the administration (Serrano 1993:120–122).

Also in 1990, OPIP increased its transnational links to San Francisco, the base for RAN. RAN began an international campaign of support for OPIP and organized international press releases and demonstrations against ARCO. RAN also published the results of an environmental impact study of the OPIP area which denounced ARCO. In August 1991, ARCO asked for a meeting with RAN to debate the results of the RAN study. In this meeting, ARCO presented the results of another environmental impact study of Block 10, which contradicted those of RAN. As a result, OPIP proposed an independent study by the Center for Environmental Design Research of the University of California (CEDR), which ARCO and RAN accepted.

In March 1992, OPIP, ARCO, RAN, and Oxfam America met again in Berkeley to analyze the independent study results. CEDR concluded that ARCO's plan for the site was excellent but not without environmental impact and gave a list of six suggestions for improvements in the ARCO plan. ARCO accepted the criticisms and agreed to continue a dialogue with OPIP to prevent future conflicts. It also proposed another meeting in California with the same actors for June 1992 to discuss a second environmental evaluation.

OPIP continued political action. On April 11, 1992, OPIP organized a march in honor of the 500 years of the discovery of the Americas (or from their point of view, the repression of indigenous peoples) from Puyo in the Oriente to Quito of about 10,000 Quichua, Achuar, and Shiwiar peoples funded by Oxfam America and a grant from the Rainforest Action Network (RAN) of $20,000, among other NGO contributions (RAN Protect-an-Acre 1995). In response to the protest, the Borja administration negotiated a land settlement with OPIP, granting their constituents 1,115,574 hectares of land, but without subsoil rights. Again, this march, international support, and the land demarcation strengthened the organization and mobilization of OPIP.

In 1992, OPIP formed the Amazanga Institute, which provides a facility for negotiation between ARCO and OPIP representatives. The Amazanga Institute, which is semi-autonomous from OPIP, combines Western and traditional technical support and research to develop environmental management plans for the Amazon, including satellite technology. The future goal of the Institute is to act as the technical/environmental consultant for all of the Amazonian indigenous communities. Thus, the Institute is working with the oil industry to place environmental monitors in their areas and to train indigenous peoples to monitor their communities. In this case as well, OPIP has utilized the influence and resources of INGOs and ARCO to affect policy change in their region. They have also combined the international environmental discourse and monitoring techniques of INGOs with the business and technical knowledge of oil MNCs.

OPIP and ARCO also have been engaged in dialogue to establish guidelines for further drilling of their land. In April 1992, a reserve of 700 million barrels of light crude was discovered in their territory (Seventh Generation Fund 1994:1–3; Villamil 1995:354–356). In response to this discovery, OPIP and ARCO representatives met again in September 1993 to discuss the development of these new drilling sites. Thus, OPIP does not solely react to the activities of ARCO, but rather independently initiates conversations and suggests solutions to joint problems.

In December 1993, OPIP called a general meeting at an oil well in Villano, the operating base of ARCO, to protest ARCO's activities. About 400 members camped out in Villano for two nights. ARCO representatives met with indigenous leaders, thus affirming the strength of OPIP in the region. As a result of this meeting, Suzana Sawyer observed that "OPIP leadership and community members began to re-articulate the relations between multinationals and local communities and influence the particular pattern of resource extraction in their territory" (1996:27).

After the Villano meeting, ARCO invited four representatives of OPIP to meet with company executives in Dallas. The goal of this meeting was not just to discuss past events, but also future events, inasmuch as the Ecuadorian government had begun its seventh round of international licensing for blocks of land in the Amazon. As a result of this meeting, OPIP and ARCO agreed that ARCO would finance and complete two studies: one on the impacts of development and the other on socio-economic impacts. As of mid-1998, this study had not been completed because ARCO had not received permission yet from the Ministry of Energy and Mines to build the pipeline that it needs for oil production.

Sixto Méndez, former Manager of the Environment, Health, and Safety for ARCO, also noted that ARCO has invested in many social programs in Pastaza community, such as medical clinics, providing nurses and doctors, potable water, cattle-selling, and investment in Amazonian artisanship. ARCO's second phase of community development is to offer two university scholarships each year to Puyo residents and it has already placed more teachers in the school system. Méndez commented that ARCO has often more influence than the municipal governments with regard to getting results from government programs. For instance, ARCO requested vaccinations from the Ministry of Health for the Pastaza province. He stated, "The government does not exist for indigenous peoples in this area" (Interview, January 19, 1997).

Méndez also noted that the Ministry of Energy and Mines is very inconsistent and thus makes working in Ecuador difficult. The minister changes so rapidly that there is no consistency in policies. The other problem that he noted was that the three local indigenous organizations in Pastaza did not agree, which also made consistent policies difficult. However, to prevent inconsistency and conflict, ARCO created a Technical/Environmental Committee, which met once a month and includes one member from Petro Ecuador, one from ARCO, and two members from each of the three local indigenous confederations. This committee acts as a forum to outline projects and create development strategies.

Despite negotiations and communication, OPIP has continued its mobilization against oil development, such as the seizure of ARCO oil wells in the Lago Agrio area, near the Yasuní Reserve, in April 1995 (*Energy Economist* 1995: 14). As recent as July 28, 1997, OPIP asked for a moratorium on oil development in their region (*El Comercio* 1997:A10).

OPIP increased its contacts with transnational actors since its inception in 1977. ARCO also included OPIP in their policymaking processes, legitimating the political role of OPIP. Since ARCO directly negotiated with OPIP, OPIP's organization and resources (transnationally and nationally) strengthened. The change in MNC behavior and exchange of information with INGOs led OPIP to change its mobilization strategies. It demanded direct contact with ARCO representatives. It also developed sophisticated facilities for researching oil development in the Amazon. OPIP cultivated international newsletters and information dissemination through international NGOs, such as the RAN, Seventh Generation Fund, Oxfam America, the Inter-American Foundation, and the Coalition for Amazonian Peoples and their Environment. Aside from inclusion within the oil policy process, OPIP obtained land rights to its territory, and held executive posts in the national indigenous organization, CONAIE, both of which further strengthened its position in negotiations with oil MNEs and within the national policy process. Since 1999, ARCO has divided its resources between Blocks 10 and 24 with Burlington Resources and Agip.

The case of OPIP is not just an instance of the mobilization of a social movement, but an illustration of the significance of private authority in the global arena. Indigenous organizations recognize the resources to be gained from international and national NGOs, but also recognize the level of power to be gained through negotiations and programs with MNCs. OPIP notes that from 1992 through 1995 it chose not to organize on a national level, but went directly to international levels. OPIP is currently planning to establish a global organization, based in Pastaza, but spanning outward with representatives in other international cities.

Phase III: Oxy (1996–1999)

Occidental Petroleum (Oxy) entered the Ecuadorian Amazon in 1985 in Block 15 in the Northeastern section of the region. This section is the home of Quichua, Siona, and Secoya indigenous peoples. Oxy exemplifies a more recent development in the history of transnational networks in the Amazon. Although Oxy began seismic testing in 1985, it stopped testing until 1993, when they re-started exploration. Before resuming testing in Limoncocha, Oxy developed a "Plan for the Communities" in 1992. In July 1996, Oxy initiated a plan for seismic testing in the more southern areas of Block 15. The initiation of this testing began the third phase of transnational networks in the Amazon, with strategies learned from previous experiences of other organizations, and new transnational movement organization techniques as well.

The Siona indigenous confederation, ONISE, and the Secoya indigenous confederation, OISE, reside in the same areas and combine mobilization strategies. The Quichua indigenous confederation of this block, FOISE (The Indigenous Organization of Sucumbíos, Ecuador) does not coordinate strategies with the other two groups. While all three groups are members of the regional organization, CONFENIAE, and share the same Amazonian identity, they do not agree on oil development within this area. Thus, the Siona and Secoya organizations have protested against development with the aid of INGOs and TSMOs, and direct negotiation with Oxy. FOISE, on the other hand, has rejected all aid and resources from INGOs or national NGOs, and directly negotiates with Oxy.

Anticipating oil development in their region, the Siona and Secoya organizations met with RAN, Center for Economic and Social Rights (CESR), and Acción Ecológica to consult their transnational partners how to negotiate a contract with an oil MNC. Thus, the Sionas and Secoyas began their mobilization in a pro-active manner, unlike the previously studied groups.

However, on July 9, 1996, the Siona and Secoya organizations argue that Oxy entered their territory, asking for permission to initiate seismic testing, with aggressive force from the Ecuadorian military. On that day, both organizations signed an accord approving seismic testing in return for water pumps, solar panels, and the chance of work for community members. By August 1996, the Sionas and Secoyas had organized against the agreement with Oxy, stating that they were unaware of the consequences and reject the agreement.

In response to their rejection of the agreement, the Sionas and Secoyas orchestrated an international strike against Oxy in Quito, Ecuador and Los Angeles, California, with the aid of RAN, Acción Ecológica, the Coalition for Amazonian Peoples and their Environment, and CESR. Moreover, RAN and the Coalition for Amazonian Peoples and their Environment mailed newsletters about their situation and contacted Oxy officials in Quito and Los Angeles. In November 1996, Shannon Wright of RAN and Chris Jochnik of CESR visited the Oxy office in Quito to request information on the Oxy activities in the Siona/Secoya region. Thus, almost immediately, the Sionas and Secoyas initiated direct contact and transnational mobilization against Oxy (Amazon Update #16 August 1996; Alerta Verde September 1996; World Rainforest Report 1996).[14]

Unlike their neighbors, FOISE had a very different experience and relationship with Oxy. Johnson Cerda, one of the leaders of FOISE, commented that FOISE did not coordinate efforts at all with NGOs or INGOs. In the past, FOISE had worked with RAN, Oxfam America, and Acción Ecológica, but now they prefer to work directly with the oil companies. He referred to the NGOs as "too extreme" in their viewpoints and negotiation techniques.

Johnson explains that Oxy invited FOISE leaders to Lago Agrio to discuss development in the Limoncocha area. The community decided to accept the Oxy plans of a highway in their community because it would bring commerce. FOISE also negotiated motors, buses, basketball courts, schools, and a 70 million sucre plan for the pavement of the roads. FOISE and Oxy negotiated appropriate rules for Oxy employees in their area, such as no alcohol and the termination of any employee that insults or threatens Quichua peoples. While FOISE would like to participate directly in the company, they are satisfied with their negotiations. Johnson even commented that "Oxy is more reliable than the government, which never does anything for Quichua people of this region" (Interview, November 12, 1996). Thus, FOISE has rejected transnational networking with NGOs in favor of direct negotiations with Oxy.

Oxy also notes that the "state does not exist" in Block 15 of the Amazon[15]. In their design of "Community Relations," Oxy is the mediator between local and national governments and the indigenous communities. "Community Relations" consists of four components: (1) infrastructure, (2) education, (3) self-development, and (4) health. Since 1992, Oxy has built four communal houses, three basketball courts, three communal dining areas, four parks, three bridges, eleven primary schools, three health clinics, one house for doctors, and one high school. These projects were completed in Siona/Secoya and Quichua areas. Manual Echeverría,

Manager of the Community Relations program, commented that he views his role as the "facilitator with the government" for indigenous communities. While in his office for an interview, two representatives of Siona/Secoya communities presented artwork for a future exposition of Siona/Secoya culture in the Oxy building. Oxy is also sponsoring a book of oral traditions of the Siona/Secoya people.[16] Thus, Siona/Secoya groups utilize direct negotiation and transnational networks to control the development of oil in their region.

The case of Oxy signals various developments in contentious transnational collective action in the Amazon. First, oil companies have learned to act as "facilitators" between state institutions and indigenous communities. Second, transnational social movement organizations have formed to mobilize across state boundaries simultaneously. Third, indigenous organizations are divided among themselves due to the quantity of international actors that have appeared in the Amazon and offer them resources. In this last case, the Siona/Secoyas and FOISE do not agree on seismic testing in their Block. While both are consulted by Oxy before acting, which is a major change from the Texaco case, and while both have professionalized their strategies, they have not coordinated them. Thus, at the same time organizations are transnationalizing, they are de-centralizing locally, regionally, and nationally.

CONCLUSIONS: THE FUTURE OF TRANSNATIONAL CONTENTIOUS COLLECTIVE ACTION?

Indigenous confederations in the Ecuadorian Amazon have altered their collective action strategies and framing to incorporate "green" ideas and discourse from INGOs, as well as business and negotiation strategies from oil MNCs. In the era of Texaco oil development, indigenous confederations and INGOs were not included at all in the policy process. However, due to transnational networks and transnational social movement organizations, the petroleum policy process in the Amazon has changed to include indigenous organizations and INGOs. Unlike the past, the oil MNCs now consult with indigenous organizations before starting projects and sometimes even form joint projects with indigenous confederations. Likewise, indigenous confederations have learned technical skills from oil MNCs and INGOs in order to independently manage the environmental protection of their regions. The shift in collective action to the transnational level signifies an increase for private actors. Once overlooked indigenous confederations are currently included in the policy process. Moreover, oil MNCs are acting as "facilitators" for government institutions. Thus, the state is not always an authoritative force in the Amazonian petroleum policy process and in fact, often times is absent.

Transnational networks created new environmental frames for the indigenous confederations. Collective action strategies on the transnational level were more focused on peaceful protest, newsletters, spread of information, and direct negotiation. As the transnational networks strengthened among these actors, their strategies became more pro-active, rather than reactive. In the case of Texaco, the Cofánes did not mobilize until 1993, almost twenty years after the start of oil production in their territory. In the case of OPIP, they too did not mobilize immediately, but did initiate pro-active strategies to prevent further seismic testing in their region. The Siona and Secoyas pro-actively responded to oil production in their region by inviting INGO consultants to advise them on negotiation strategies. Thus, the future of transnational contentious collective action in the Amazon is moving in a more informed and pro-active direction.

Due to transnational networks, indigenous confederations have achieved a number of policy gains on various levels. The Cofánes have gained control over their region in the Cuyabeño Reserve and must be consulted before any activity in this area. Texaco is also in the process of a billion-dollar clean-up for environmental degradation in their area. Furthermore, the Cofánes have gained international status and notoriety for their lawsuit against Texaco in New York. It remains to be seen what the outcomes of this court case will be.

OPIP has benefitted from various policy outcomes. It was awarded a land grant from the Ecuadorian government, due partly to transnational network pressures. OPIP has also designed an environmental protection plan with ARCO and has deferred further seismic testing in their area until environmental assessments show that it is safe for the population. With ARCO, OPIP has negotiated better environmental protection of the community and rivers. Moreover, ARCO has donated medical supplies, clinics, nurses and doctors, potable water, schools, and support for artisans. It has also acted as the "facilitator" for OPIP with the government, for example by pressuring the Ministry of Health for vaccinations in Pastaza. On the level of INGOs, OPIP has received various environmental and technical advice and funding from RAN and University of California, Berkeley. Thus, the policy outcomes transcend state level to transnational levels.

The Siona and Secoyas and FOISE have also benefitted from various policy outcomes. While they have not received land grants, they have negotiated sufficiently to be included in the policy process of Oxy. Oxy, also, has learned from the transnational network process to include indigenous groups in their planning and policy activities. Thus far, Oxy is the only oil company in the Amazon that includes indigenous peoples on their corporate planning committees. Moreover, Oxy and the communities have negotiated various programs and projects dealing with infrastructure, health, self-development, and education. Thus, rather than seeking outcomes from the national government, the Siona and Secoyas and FOISE have opted to negotiate on transnational levels.

These policy outcomes and negotiations signal the authority of private, non-state actors in the international system. Indigenous leaders and oil MNCs have commented that the "state does not exist" in the Amazon. Thus, they act outside of state realms to create policy change and programs. Moreover, INGOs have initiated transnational collective action strategies, which pressure various actors in various states simultaneously. The outcomes of this collective action are not always obvious on state levels, but rather derive from other sources, such as oil MNCs and INGOs.

Although indigenous confederations have benefitted from transnational networks, the future may not be so bright. As illustrated in the last case, FOISE and the Siona/Secoya groups are in disagreement with one another and have not coordinated their strategies. Rather, each organization has cooperated directly with transnational actors, Siona/Secoya with INGOs and FOISE with Oxy. Therefore, their transnational networks are very strong, but their local and regional networks and organizations have weakened. This case demonstrates the impacts of transnational networks on the organizational level.

Transnational contentious collective action may divide social movement leaders, vying for power on the transnational level, which disconnects them from the bases of their movement. Moreover, transnational networks may prevent groups from organizing beyond local level to the national level because they got resources and favorable outcomes from transnational actors without the need to coordinate forces on a national level. As noted in these cases, INGOs play a much more significant role in negotiations than do other neighboring indigenous confederations or the national indigenous confederation, CONAIE. Indeed, the national confederation and the regional Amazonian confederation (CONFENIAE) have strengthened their organizations since the initiation of transnational networks, but transnational resources may provide a source of competition and tension among social movement organizations.

Therefore, the future of transnational contentious collective action may be one of smaller, local social movement organizations linked with transnational actors, with the goal of policy outcomes on local, regional, or international levels, but possibly not from the national state. Although the indigenous movement of Ecuador has organized nationally through the political party, Pachakutik, and won Congressional delegates in the national elections, their recent election of leaders for the CONAIE (national indigenous organization) signaled a rupture between groups, ultimately ending in protests against one another. These protests occurred during the January 1997 elections of the CONAIE executive offices, where Amazonian indigenous organizations, particularly FOIN and OPIP vied for Amazonian leadership and the Sierra groups argued with Amazonian groups for control of the executive. In the end, OPIP won the executive office of President, which caused some tension between Amazonian organizations and OPIP, and the Amazon and the Sierra organizations. However, since January 1997, the CONAIE has consolidated its membership and leaders and has remained a political force within the national political system.

However, funding processes of INGOs and IGOs are changing, which does guide the process of transnational collective action. In interviews with every INGO working in Ecuador, each director commented on the restructuring of funding toward smaller, manageable projects on local, or base, levels. For the Ecuadorian Amazon, this may signify a turn from individual social movement organizations towards transnational mobilization, coordinated on a grand scale by transnational social movement organizations, such as COICA or the Coalition for Amazonian Peoples and their Environment. Therefore, while the globalization of social movement organizations may expand strategies of mobilization to new, transnational levels, it may also decrease national, regional, and local strategy coordination.

NOTES

[1]Authority is the ability to command outcomes. As Cutler, Haufler, and Porter contend, private actor (meaning non-state actors) authority has increased due to the globalization of market forces. Thus, MNCs have assumed an authoritative role in the international system (Cutler, Claire, Virginia Haufler, and Tony Porter. *Private Authority and International Relations*. SUNY Press:1999). Included in the definition of private actors are also societal actors, in this case, indigenous peoples. While influence is an indirect form of obtaining outcomes, authority signals a command and direct ability to change outcomes. As noted in Chapter 2, this study will refer to authority in these terms.

[2]For references to each of these social movements and their transnational links, see Alison Brysk (1994, 1994, and 1995); Margaret Keck and Katherine Sikkink (1995); Ronnie D. Lipschutz (1992); Thomas Princen and Matthias Finger,eds. (1994); Kathryn Sikkink (1993); and Paul Wapner (1995).

[3]For example, see James Rosenau (1992); Paul Wapner (1996) James Riker (1995 and 1996); Philip Cerny (1995); M.J. Peterson (1992); and Ronnie D. Lipschutz (1992).

[4]A point noted by Sidney Tarrow (1994 and 1996); Jackie Smith (1994); and Thomas Risse-Kappen (1995).

[5]INEC (Instituto Ecuatoriano de Censos y Estadísticas); V Censo de Poblacíon y IV de Vivienda 1990. Quito, INEC, 1991. See also, Ortiz, Pablo and Anamaría Varea (1995). "Amazonia: Características Generales y Conflictos." In Varea, Anamaría, ed. *Marea Negra en la Amazonia*. Quito, Ediciones Abya-Yala.

[6]This statistic varies according to sources. Some sources estimate that the indigenous population is closer to 85,000. See Ortiz, Pablo and Anamaría Varea (1995). "Amazonia: Características y Conflictos." In Varea, Anamaría, ed. *Marea Negra en la Amazonia*. Quito, Ediciones Abya-Yala:pp.39.

[7]I estimate 120,000 people because exact numbers of these groups have not been surveyed. The numbers in parentheses are approximations based on academic studies.

[8]Ortiz, Pablo and Anamaría Varea (1995). "Amazonia: Caraterísticas y Conflictos" In Varea, Anamaría. *Marea Negra en la Amazonia*. Quito, Ediciones Abya-Yala:pp.49–51.

[9]The current organization of the Siona is ONISE, or the Organization of Siona Indigenous Nationalities of Ecuador. The current organization of the Secoya is OISE, or the Organization of Secoya Indigenous Nationalities of Ecuador. These two groups do coordinate organizational and mobilizational efforts, but no longer as a single organization.

[10]See, Coalition for Amazonian Peoples and their Environment (February 1997), Director Melina Selverston. Washington, D.C. "General Information;" and Chase Smith, Richard (1996). "La Política de la diversidad. COICA y las federaciones étnicas de la Amazonía" Quito, Ediciones Abya-Yala.

[11]Interview, March 7, 1997. Leonardo Viteri, Technical Consultant of OPIP and President, Amazanga Institute.

[12]Interview, March 10, 1997. Hans Hoffmeyer, Director, IBIS-Denmark.

[13]Interview, January 19, 1997. Sixto Méndez, Manager Environmental, Health, and Safety, ARCO Oriente, Inc.

[14]Information from this section was also derived from an interview with Shannon Wright of RAN, November 16, 1996.

[15]Interview with Manuel Echeverria, Engineer and Manager of the Community Relations Program, Occidental Oil Company, November 20, 1996.

[16]This information was also provided through an interview with Manuel Echeverría, November 20, 1996.

CHAPTER FIVE

Transnational Social Movements: COICA[1] and the Coalition for Amazonian Peoples and Their Environment

INTRODUCTION

THE SOUTH AMERICAN AMAZON IS CONNECTED VIA TRANSNATIONAL advocacy networks and transnational social movement organizations (TSMOs). In the previous chapter, I focused on the transnational advocacy networks of INGOs, oil companies, indigenous confederations, and the Ecuadorian state to demonstrate the impacts of transnational actors on contentious politics on domestic and international levels. Transnational advocacy networks differ from transnational social movements in that transnational social movements are "sustained interactions with opponents based on the claims of connected networks of challengers organized on the basis of collective interests and values across national boundaries" (Tarrow 1998: 414). As described in chapter 2, transnational social movements include a high level of embedded collective identities and common purposes, or depth, and a high level of links and communications among transnational and domestic actors, or breadth. Transnational advocacy networks also share high levels of links and communications, but their collective identities and common purposes differ among actors transnationally and domestically. As Tarrow explains, transnational social movements may change their targets and goals, yet they still share "common ways of seeing the world,... and are connected to one another across national boundaries more than episodically" (Tarrow 1998: 414). Thus, transnational social movements are the highest level of transnational contentious collective action in the model used for this project.

This chapter explores the characteristics and functions of TSMOs and the challenges that they pose to their targets via an analysis of their strategies, organization, mobilization, and outcomes. Most examples of TSMOs in the literature are based primarily in industrialized, developed countries, such as Greenpeace and Friends of the Earth (Wapner 1996; Tarrow 1996;1998). However, the two TSMOs presented in this chapter are organized by indigenous actors and Amazonian activists and are based and develop their strategies in South American Amazonian countries. At first glance, it may seem unlikely that these resource-challenged actors could organize on such a grand scale. The mere fact that this has occurred makes the analysis of these TSMOs even more provocative.

THEORETICAL FRAMEWORK

As mentioned in chapter 2, TSMOs utilize various tools of organizing and mobilizing to sustain their networks and increase their effectiveness. One of the most important of these tools is the social networks and identities of group members. In the case of *transnational* social movements, space, or distance, has been the recurring challenge for researchers who approach their analysis from the perspective of domestic social movements. Sidney Tarrow (1998) has suggested that this space between actors, which is normally not present in domestic social movements, may be made less significant via the concept of "social capital," which was developed by Robert Putnam in his 1994 book, *Making Democracy Work*. Putnam referred to the organizational and social ties between Northern and Southern Italians, which he found significant in the implementation of democratic institutions. However, Tarrow has utilized this concept to include organizational and social ties among transnational social movement members. Whereas Putnam referred to football organizations and church groups, which are locally based, Tarrow has moved this concept to the transnational realm of e-mail, fax, and international travel, thus shortening the supposed gap of space between individuals. This new version of "social capital" developed by Tarrow permits us to analyze a TSMO and its ability to have common purposes, identities, and social networks through a new vision of space which is overcome by modern means of communication and travel.

For example, both COICA and the Coalition[2] have utilized modern means of communication to overcome the spatial gap among members. Both TSMOs send daily faxes, e-mails, and phone calls to one another. In addition, they organize bi-annual meetings, where all representatives are present. They have furthermore reported meeting with one another as often as once every month to mobilize various campaigns and distribute new information. Both TSMOs of the South American Amazon claim the indigenous Amazonian heritage as their common identity. Their common purpose, or way of seeing the world, has always been the environmental protection of the Amazon, which includes protection of its lands, rivers, social customs, and rights of the indigenous peoples. Thus, their social capital, while not developed via spatially close social ties, does exist and is coherent among various groups across national boundaries.

Another important element, or tool, of the organization and mobilization of TSMOs is *framing*. Frames are ways in which movement organizations present themselves and their issues to others and to the members of the organization in order to motivate and legitimate the movement (McAdam 1996: 339). The process of framing includes the use of symbols and ideas that are significant in various political cultures. Frames, according to David Snow (1988), can be transferred to other movements, or they can become a part of the larger political culture. Social movement organizations utilize *master frames* under which movement specific-frames may form. In the case of the Amazon, TSMO leaders chose the master frame of "the environment" and "sustainable development," under which they have developed Amazonian-specific frames to mobilize local and regional groups. For example, the umbrella, or master frame, of the environment is broad enough to include the Amazonian-specific frame of indigenous peoples and their ways of living as part of the environment, or ecological composition of the Amazon. Therefore, the protection of the Amazonian ecosystem also signifies the protection of its indigenous peoples.

The tools of domestic social movements— networks, identities, and frames—are also applicable in the transnational realm. As often cited in the literature of domestic social movements, these organizations grow by the strengthening of social networks. In this chapter, I claim that the South American TSMOs, COICA and the Coalition, grew out of the strengthening of transnational advocacy networks that had existed for many years. Moreover, the issue networks that formed through these years of organizing aided in the formation of the common Amazonian indigenous identity. Thus, the transnational advocacy networks examined in the previous chapter are an important part of the explanation of the development of the TSMOs analyzed in this chapter.

CASE OVERVIEW

The TSMOs analyzed in this chapter are the only two existing TSMOs focused exclusively on the Amazon. COICA is South American-based and is an organization whose members are solely South American indigenous peoples. The Coalition is Washington D.C.-based and has a membership of all COICA members, as well as other INGOs with shared visions of the world. COICA was founded in 1984 and has grown and changed since that time. The Coalition was recently founded, with the aid of COICA, in 1994. While COICA focuses its efforts more on South American issues and international institutions, the Coalition tends to focus its mobilization more broadly, such as lobbying the U.S. Congress and applying for World Bank funding for Amazonian projects. Although both organizations coordinate strategies, they are two separate TSMO's with slightly different goals. The rest of this chapter will examine the histories of formation of the these TSMO's, their organizational structures, strategies, and framing processes, as well as analyze the issues around which they mobilize.

I. Organizational Structure—COICA

COICA is an organization very well connected to its counterparts in other South American countries. COICA includes the Amazonian confederations of Peru, Guyana, Bolivia, Brazil, Ecuador, Venezuela, French Guyana, Surinam, and Colombia, and claims to represent over four hundred indigenous communities in the Amazon basin. These indigenous communities are 70 percent of the total population of the Amazon, and 100 percent of its politically organized population. COICA members accept the Amazonian indigenous ethnicity as their common identity and have affirmed this through various coordinated marches, literature, discourse, and communications.

COICA is composed of representative organizations in each of its member countries. These organizations inform members of COICA activities and coordinate COICA activities at the local and regional levels. Aside from these organizations, COICA organizes a Congress every four years to detail objectives, review previous activities, and formulate new goals based on member needs. This Congress takes place in a member-state and consists of ten members from each member-state who have equal voting rights.

Although the Congress is useful in organizing overall goals, COICA utilizes the Coordination Council to plan budgetary expenses, develop policies out of the Congressional goals, and confront any problems or crisis situations. The Council meets every six months and consists of the presidents of each organization and two delegates. From these policies, the Directive Council, which is composed of the four organizers of each policy area, executes specific policy goals and informs presidents in each member-state of their activities. The Directive Council currently resides in the Quito-based headquarters of the organization. Aside from these official organizational meetings, according to COICA technical advisor, Rodrigo de la Cruz, members often meet in international conferences sponsored by COICA, so that on average, members meet four to five times a year.

Based on the Congress of 1996, which set the organizational goals until 2000, COICA members are focusing on four areas: 1) the environment, 2) protection and demarcation of territories, 3) autonomous economic development, and 4) the protection of human rights. COICA does not implement projects on a local level. Rather, it focuses on the overall Amazonian regional level, creating programs and conferences that unite members and fortify common goals. Moreover, COICA has participated in and completed various studies of the region, funded by the United Nations, Oxfam America, and Climate Alliance. Thus, COICA's organizational structure relies on heavy interaction among member-state leaders and frequent visits between COICA leaders in Quito and member-states (COICA Interview 1997).

II. The History of COICA

Although COICA officially was founded in 1984, its history can be traced to the transnational networks, which began to form in the Amazon in the 1960s. During this time period, many missionaries traveled to the Amazon, teaching Christianity and translating the Bible into the various indigenous languages. These were, in many instances, the first contacts that indigenous peoples had with "outsiders." Between 1960 and 1964, the Summer Institute of Linguistics, a missionary group dedicated to bilingual education, began to develop its programs in the Peruvian and Ecuadorian Amazonian regions. Before the arrival of these missionary groups and the Summer Institute of Linguistics, most indigenous groups remained organized on a local, community level, but not on a political level. However, these Western-organized missionary groups not only brought with them religious teachings, they also helped organize the indigenous groups into political confederations. These were the first transnational networks formed in the Amazon basin.

Aside from missionaries, anthropologists, and other academics also aided in the development of indigenous organizations and transnational networks. The protests of anthropologists worldwide were in response to the economic development of the Amazon basin, such as mineral drilling, petroleum development and seismic testing, and agro-industry. It was the transnational links with anthropologists and missionaries that primarily lead to the transnationalization of the Amazonian indigenous rights movement.

In 1971, the Catholic Church sponsored a meeting of anthropologists in Barbados to analyze the situation of indigenous communities in the Amazon basin. They sought to liberate indigenous people from their colonial situation and began to organize transnational funding for projects. In

1977, anthropologists met again in Barbados to analyze the situation, but this time with indigenous representatives. This meeting spurred social networks among INGO members and indigenous leaders from all over South America.

During the 1970s, as social networks and communications grew between INGO members and South American indigenous peoples, various transnational organizations developed. By the end of the 1970s, the International Working Group for Indigenous Peoples (IWGIA), was established in Copenhagen. Survival International, an INGO dedicated to the prevention of abuses against indigenous peoples, formed in London. Cultural Survival, an INGO sponsored by Harvard University, was initiated with the goal of aiding Amazonian indigenous peoples to protect their cultures and lands, while adapting to new economic and social conditions in their countries. Finally, in 1982, the United Nations, through the Commission on Human Rights in the Economic and Social Council, developed the Working Group for Indigenous Peoples, giving them consultative status within the UN. Each of these transnational organizations created new opportunities for indigenous peoples from the Amazon basin to communicate, share experiences, and form closer social networks. At the same time, the global community was becoming more aware of the campaign of Amazonian indigenous peoples through INGOs predominantly based in the United States and Europe.

The impetus for the foundation of COICA began in 1984 through an international conference of five Amazonian countries (Peru, Ecuador, Brazil, Columbia, and Venezuela) in Lima, Peru, sponsored by the United Nations Working Group for Indigenous Peoples. The purpose of this conference was to establish a common terminology for all Amazonian indigenous peoples and common strategies to confront problems of the recognition of rights and territorial issues. Finally, it was decided, among the indigenous representatives present, that the common identity would be of "Pueblos Indígenas," or "Indigenous Communities." The idea behind this decision was their common understanding that all indigenous peoples of the Amazon were one whole community bound by the commitment to defend their collective lands and rights.

III. Forming Transnational Political Strategies

The international political actions of COICA began in the Working Group of the United Nations. Each year after 1982, new representatives from all Amazonian countries would participate in the group, learning political strategies, making contacts with INGO representatives, and forming tighter bonds among themselves. In 1985, COICA joined the campaign to pass Agreement 169 of the International Labor Organization, which protects the rights of workers. Through this campaign, COICA members made contacts with the Green Party of Europe and various European workers' unions. These new European contacts funded various trips for COICA members to travel to Europe to campaign about Amazonian indigenous rights.

Moreover, in 1986, COICA gained international recognition when it won the Right Livelihood Prize for human rights protection. Three representatives from COICA traveled from South America to Washington,D.C., Boston, Stockholm, and London for a press tour to gain recognition of the honor. During these tours, COICA representatives met Barber Conable, then-President of the World Bank. This began discussions between COICA leaders and the World Bank for the funding of various projects in the Amazon.

From 1988 until 1992, COICA not only developed its communication skills but began projects with funding from various INGOs. These projects eventually developed the master frame that COICA would utilize: the environment. In conjunction with Oxfam America, Survival International, and Esopus Creek Communications, COICA developed a program of providing information, press materials, and speeches to most environmental NGOs in the United States about the indigenous point of view of ecology and preservation of lands. Following this tour of the United States, COICA organized a conference in Iquitos, Peru on the environment in order to combine strategies and exchange ideas between U.S. environmental NGOs and COICA. This conference initiated various environmental programs in the Amazon, such as a study of the economic development of indigenous peoples who utilize traditional forms of land development, sponsored by Oxfam America and the World Bank (Smith 1996:104–113). This study has published two books: one is an analysis of the results, and the other is a textbook about indigenous cultures and forms of traditional economic development, utilized in school systems in indigenous areas.

Following its first three years of master frame development around the environment, COICA again gained recognition for its efforts by winning the Goldman Prize for the Environment. Then-President Evaristo Nugkuag traveled to the United States and Europe on a press tour to present Amazonian ideas of environmental protection and sustainable development. The funding from this award, and aid from Oxfam America, was utilized to establish communications systems among the Amazonian headquarters to better communicate between COICA members. At that time, fax machines were the primary mode of communication chosen by COICA representatives. However, currently, COICA members utilize e-mail as another source of communication. Thus, the early days of organization and mobilization of COICA were centered upon political strategy development and master frame development. COICA built its initial contacts with U.S. and European environmental INGOs in order to 1) spread the Amazonian conception of environmental protection and sustainable development, 2) create funding lines and projects between INGOs and COICA, and 3) to insert the specific Amazonian indigenous peoples' frame into the larger master frame of the environment, and to a lesser extent, human rights.

IV. Issues and Political Strategies

Nineteen ninety-three was an important year not just for COICA but for all indigenous peoples of the world. This particular year was declared "Year of Indigenous Peoples" by the United Nations, facilitated by the Working Group for Indigenous Peoples, of which COICA is a member. COICA also consolidated its organization in 1993. After years of organizing through meetings in various Amazonian cities, COICA decided to establish a base in Quito where all its activities would be coordinated. Furthermore, representatives from various member-states would reside in Quito for one year to collaborate with other members and disperse information to their home-state members. The inauguration of the COICA office in Quito was accompanied by a meeting of over two hundred Amazonian indigenous peoples to discuss the future plans and coordination of the organization (*Punto de Vista* 1993: 6–7).

The formation of a regional office also inspired new forms of mobilization. In order to disperse information about its activities and update members about other COICA locations, leaders established a magazine called *Our Amazon*. This magazine includes contributions about activities in all COICA member-states such as meetings, new challenges, outcomes of campaigns, and future plans. Moreover, the magazine is sent to over five hundred INGOs worldwide to communicate Amazonian ideas and activities. Contributions to the magazine are generally sent through e-mail correspondence and it includes an e-mail address for comments or subscriptions. Oxfam America, IBIS Denmark, and the U.N. WORKING GROUP make funding for the magazine possible for Indigenous Peoples. Thus, COICA had consolidated its organizational base, as well as developed a form of information dissemination for members as well as INGO donors and actors.

Since 1993, COICA has developed a complex form of transnational political strategy to alert members and supporters of its campaigns. At its base in Quito, COICA has established an office of communications and press to send press releases and communicate with members about problems and outcomes. During frequent visits to this office, I witnessed the press consultant, Rodolfo Azar, receive frequent phone calls and faxes related to press campaigns and issue-areas in member countries. Moreover, the President Valerio Grefa received numerous phone calls from INGO participants and indigenous members organizing various campaigns. Grefa spoke with familiarity, as he would to a friend, to the large majority of indigenous members and INGO participants. The common ties that Grefa has with other members and the activity of the press office signal high levels of communication and interaction among COICA members.

This section of the chapter analyzes various COICA campaigns and their political strategies. The majority of information for this section was collected from the COICA archives in Quito, observation, and interviews.

YANOMAMIS IN BRAZIL

In August 1993 it was discovered that ten Yanomami children, five women, and two men were murdered and decapitated by gold miners near Brazil's border with Venezuela. After the event, Yanomami leaders alerted the COICA headquarters in Quito of the details and asked them to begin a campaign against the mineral resource extraction community of the Amazon, as well as directly against the Brazilian government. According to COICA archival information and Yanomami reports (as well as corroborated information by INGOs, such as Amnesty International), the Yanomami community has suffered from attacks against their members for years by resource extraction companies, with little or no support from their government. In one communiqué from the Yanomami office to COICA, the Yanomamis state that their "only voice to the global community is through COICA" (COICA archive 1993). Thus, the Yanomami community mounted its campaign against the violation of the rights of its community through COICA.

In order to mobilize its members, COICA first sent an e-mail message to member leaders to consult their opinions and coordinate strategies. COICA commonly uses fax and e-mail messages to advise members of new, important issues. Although COICA does have a governing body located in Quito, it frequently utilizes group decision-making techniques before acting, which are common in Amazonian indigenous cultures.

Once all members were alerted and conferred with, COICA began a massive press campaign against the Brazilian government and gold-miners in the Amazon. Articles were sent, via the COICA Communications Office, to journals and INGO newsletters, reporting the fatalities and denouncing resource extraction in the Amazon. One article sent as a general press

release, and later published in the Ecuadorian NGO international journal
Acción Ecológica, stated that:

> Indigenous peoples constitute the air, the forest, the land, which may
> seem romantic, but it is the truth. What we feel in our souls and our
> bodies is a unity with Mother Earth. It is a natural alliance...
> Indigenous communities conserve, protect, and live with Mother Earth.
> If people remove us from the land, they are removing the defense of the
> environment as well. If people kill an indigenous person, they are
> killing the environment and, more than that, our knowledge of the
> environment, which is so important to the world community. (COICA
> July 21, 1993).

COICA "framed" the crime against Yanomamis in Brazil as a crime against
humanity due to the resource extraction industry's destruction not only of
the flora and fauna, but of the human life which protects the knowledge of
them. Moreover, COICA highlights the importance of Amazonian peoples
not only for the Amazon, but for all people of the world,. Thus, the deaths
of seventeen Yanomami peoples were translated into crimes not only
against the Yanomamis, but against all peoples of the world.

Aside from press releases to journals and newspapers, as well as e-
mails, COICA sent letters to the Organization of American States, the
United Nations Commission on Human Rights, and the Brazilian government. These letters were directed towards the issues of violations of human
rights and violations of the protection of indigenous lands and the "irre-
sponsible extraction of world resources" (COICA July 1993). Thus,
COICA, aside from mobilizing via INGOs, also directly acts against member-state governments and policies.

The Yanomami issue was also combined with the issue of implementing a system of laser surveillance in the Amazon. The Brazilian military had proposed a system of lasers to prevent drug trafficking in the
Amazonian region. The governments of Venezuela and Colombia had also
publicly offered their support for this $1 billion project. COICA protested
in Quito against this system, claiming that the Brazilian government
"should spend the money on projects for sustainable development...
because the Amazon is the principal fountain of life for all humanity"
(COICA July 21, 1993). This campaign included the lives of indigenous
peoples as a global natural resource, and part of the sustainable development of the Amazon, and the world.

Following the COICA campaign against the Brazilian government,
two gold-miners in the Yanomami territory were arrested and imprisoned.
Furthermore, an investigation into the processes of mineral extraction in

the Yanomami territory was initiated by COICA with international funding. The two men arrested for killing seventeen Yanomamis were freed from prison after four months. COICA was displeased with this ruling, and sent a follow-up letter to the Brazilian government in response.

ASHANINKAS IN PERU

Like Brazil, Peru has experienced killings of its Amazonian peoples. In September 1994, the Peruvian branch of COICA alerted the Quito office that fifty-six Ashaninkas were murdered by the guerrilla group, Sendero Luminoso (Shining Path). The 10,000 Ashaninkan people claim that Sendero Luminoso has been utilizing their territory and has forced them to move to another part of the Amazon. The Peru office of COICA requested an international campaign against Sendero Luminoso and the Peruvian government on behalf of the Ashaninkas.

As in the Brazilian case, the Quito office of COICA alerted other COICA members of the crisis in Peru via fax and e-mail. Following this communication, an international press release was sent to all major news sources and to the Organization of American States Inter-American Commission on Human Rights. Articles were written by Ashaninkas about their experiences and were published in the COICA magazine, *Our Amazon*. COICA also sent a file to the OAS on behalf of the Ashaninkas, including information and testimony. One year later, three Ashaninkas testified before the OAS Commission in Washington, D.C. about their experiences and violations of human rights. This trip was funded by COICA (COICA Archives November 11, 1994).

The case of the Ashaninkas in Peru was often combined with the murder of Yanomamis in Brazil and "framed" as a loss of "indigenous knowledge and biodiversity" which supports the entire Amazonian ecosystem (COICA Archives November 11, 1994). In one press release, the COICA president, Valerio Grefa, wrote that the situation in Peru was "comparable to that of Rwanda" in terms of violations of human rights and deaths (COICA Archives September 5, 1994). Thus, COICA utilized already accepted international frames and cases of human rights to highlight the urgency of their campaign in the Ashaninka region of Peru to the rest of the international community.

FREE TRADE IN THE AMERICAS

Unlike the crisis situation cases of the Yanomamis and the Ashaninkas, the campaign against Free Trade in the Americas was organized and mobilized by all COICA member-states. On November 28– 30, 1994, COICA, the

Chilean Mapuches' Council for all the Land and the Association Kuna Napguana from Panama organized an international conference in Bogota, Colombia, for indigenous peoples to analyze the facets of and effects of free trade on indigenous peoples in Latin America. The argument from COICA president, Valerio Grefa, was that the American presidents had not considered their indigenous populations in the designing, or the implementation, of the free trade agreement (COICA Archive November 12, 1994).

COICA, in order to capture international attention for the conference, also organized the signing of the U.N. Treaty proclaiming "The Decade of Indigenous Populations of the World." Thus, COICA utilized the agenda of the U.N. document signing to launch its conference in Bogotá about free trade.

Aside from the strategy of organizing an international conference, COICA also drafted and sent a letter to all American presidents, outlining the demands of indigenous peoples ("Carta Abierta a los Presidentes Americanos," November 30, 1994). These demands included: the recognition of indigenous rights, participation in democratic processes, the right to education in their indigenous languages and cultures, the preservation of natural resources, and the right to sustainable economic development in accordance with indigenous economic means (COICA December 5, 1994).

Following the conference in Bogotá, COICA sent a letter to the Summit of American leaders in Miami in December 1994, expressing the opinions of indigenous leaders. In this case, COICA did not choose a master frame, but rather utilized the master frame of free trade as its target. While the process of free trade was not impeded by the efforts of COICA, the purpose of its strategy was to alert American presidents and the international community to their presence. Most major press sources did run a release of the summit in Bogotá, including Reuters, Inter-Press Services, APA, *El País* (Spain), and *El Comercio* (Ecuador). Thus, COICA was effective, not in policy outcomes, but in the dissemination of information in this case.

PEACE BETWEEN PERU AND ECUADOR

In 1995, a war broke out between Peru and Ecuador over the Amazonian border which divides these two countries. The conflict between Ecuador and Peru has been an issue since the signing of the Protocol of Rio de Janeiro in 1942, which demarcated the two countries' borders; the Protocol later was protested by Ecuador. The area in questions is shared by indigenous communities of both countries which frequently cross the border and consider themselves part of the same community and ethnic group. When war broke out, indigenous peoples were forced to take up arms against one another as directed by the militaries of both countries. However, this caused great conflict among the indigenous communities and between the indigenous communities and their respective states.

Thus, COICA, as a neutral, international representative of all Amazonian indigenous peoples, organized an international meeting of the Peruvian and Ecuadorian indigenous peoples and leaders in La Paz, Bogotá from July 16–19, 1995. The mediators for this meeting were indigenous leaders from Bolivia, Colombia, and French Guyana. The goal of the meeting was to establish strategies to create peace on the border and to work together to convince both state leaders to sign a peace agreement and end the conflict (COICA Archive July 10, 1995, July 12, 1995).

One result of this meeting was a massive press campaign to end the conflict between the two countries. COICA sent letters to the OAS, asking for support in peace talks with state leaders. COICA also utilized the legal and communication services of the Indian Law Resource Center in Washington, D.C. to intervene in peace talks. The Indian Law Resource Center, a U.S.-based INGO dedicated to aiding indigenous peoples with legal problems, contacted the National Congress of American Indians (NCAI) for help in a press campaign alerting international organization leaders, such as the United Nations and the OAS, and the presidents of Peru and Ecuador of the danger that the border conflict poses to Amazonian indigenous communities (COICA Archive February 22, 1995). During this time, COICA president, Valerio Grefa, had many telephone conversations with Armstrong Wiggins of the Indian Law Resource Center and the NCAI president, Garashkibos. Thus, interaction among these U.S.-based INGOs was close and frequent during this campaign.

The campaign resulted in an investigation by the OAS and an international conference between Peruvian and Ecuadorian indigenous peoples, with the aid of the Indian Law Resource Center, in October 1995. The goal of the campaign was to alert the leaders of both countries of their common ethnic groups in the border area and the threat to their lives. This goal was achieved through the assistance of INGOs and through the organization of indigenous leaders from Peru, Ecuador, and COICA. A peace accord between the two countries was agreed upon and approved by the Congresses of each respective country in October 1998. To this date, it is unclear what the role of COICA will be in the border demarcation process.

INTELLECTUAL PROPERTY RIGHTS

In July 1996, Loren Miller, a representative of International Plan Medicine Corporation, patented the sacred Amazonian plant, Ayahuasca, in the United States. The patenting of a traditional plant by a foreign company caused a furor in the Amazonian indigenous community. In response, COICA organized an international conference in Santa Cruz, Bolivia, to inform indigenous leaders about intellectual property rights and mechanisms to protect these rights. This conference was sponsored by the U.N. Development Program, which also provided expert consultation on the issue-area.

The campaign to protect traditional medicinal plants of the Amazon is relatively recent. It draws on the master frame of the environment by focusing on the protection of "traditional knowledge and customs" (COICA Archives June 24, 1996). While COICA began its campaign involving only Amazonian indigenous peoples, in 1997 it expanded its conferences to include indigenous representatives from Asia and Africa. Thus, COICA has focused upon a common problem, while utilizing the broader "indigenous" identity to unite people for the purpose of protecting traditional flora and fauna. COICA is continuing its actions against the patenting of Ayahuasca and has recently obtained a reversal of the original patent decision for a time period.

OIL

As analyzed in Chapter Four, COICA has been closely involved in negotiations between oil companies and indigenous confederations. COICA holds the position as a neutral mediator with the intention of assisting in gaining "favorable conditions" for indigenous peoples (COICA Interview 1997).

Moreover, COICA has utilized the Ecuadorian example to inform other indigenous organizations. It provides international consultants to aid indigenous leaders in the negotiation process. It has utilized the following strategies in this issue-area: press campaigns against oil companies; the collection of international funding and advice from IGOs and INGOs; international conferences for indigenous leaders to inform them of negotiation mechanisms and environmental consequences; meetings directly with oil company executives to create joint programs; and meetings with INGO members to coordinate programs for sustainable development.

These strategies were utilized in the cases of Maxus Oil Company and the Huaorani; Occidental and the Siona Secoya; ARCO and OPIP; and Texaco and the Cofánes. In none of these cases, did COICA play a direct role in the communities, but rather remained an observer and consultant. According to Technical Consultant Rodrigo de la Cruz, COICA members communicate daily about oil development in the Amazon. Furthermore, indigenous leaders from all COICA member-states meet on an average of four to five times a year to discuss the situation of oil development in their respective countries (COICA Interview 1997). Thus, COICA, while not directly involved in negotiation terms and outcomes, has coordinated efforts to unite and educate indigenous peoples about sustainable development and oil production.

COICA AS A TRANSNATIONAL SOCIAL MOVEMENT

COICA is a transnational social movement because it has sustained interactions with its networks and has collective interests, identities, and values that it shares across national boundaries. While the issue-areas of COICA may change based on national circumstances, the identity and purpose (breadth) of indigenous peoples is always sustained. Moreover, COICA maintains its high level of depth (or, links among members) through weekly phone calls and faxes, e-mail, and international conferences to link members and make joint decisions on future goals and strategies.

The master frame of COICA is the environment, which it uses to illustrate indigenous ideas on sustainable development and land protection. This master frame is translated into local frames in each member-state, depending on the issue-area at hand, for example, flora and fauna, oil development, or traditional medicine. Moreover, COICA shares its goals with the international community through relations with various INGOs and joint development programs. Thus, COICA has circumvented local, social networks through the use of international modes of communication and travel to create a transnational social movement.

I. Organizational Structure—The Coalition

The Coalition for Amazonian Peoples and their Environment is the Northern[3] branch of COICA in the sense that the Coalition coordinates funding, projects, conferences, and other activities between Northern environmental NGOs and funding agencies, and COICA. The Coalition is composed of some forty-five member NGOs, primarily from the United States and Europe. The Coalition is a separate transnational social movement from COICA because, although it shares goals and projects, it has a separate membership, distinct identity, different social networks, and focuses on the organization of Northern members and the coordination of these members with Amazonian, COICA members. Therefore, the Coalition acts as the "umbrella" which unites North and South under the larger identity of the environment and indigenous rights.

The Coalition's goals are defined in part by the Congress of COICA. The Coalition and COICA leaders work together to communicate common goals and initiatives, coordinating on the levels of North and South. Thus, like COICA, the Coalition's agenda includes 1) the environment, 2) defining territories for indigenous peoples, 3) human rights, and 4) sustainable development systems for indigenous peoples. The Coalition defines itself as "an organization of support organizations to cooperate in alliance with indigenous and traditional peoples of the natural ecosystems in the countries of the Amazon basin" (Annual Meeting Report 1996:24).[4] Thus, the common identity, or way of viewing the world, among members of the Coalition is that of support for indigenous peoples and their ecosystems.

The Coalition is a diverse organization of Northern NGO members and Amazonian indigenous leaders. Representing this diversity is the advisory board, or Alliance Committee, which includes five indigenous leaders and five leaders from INGOs. These members are consulted on all Coalition policies are re-elected every two years. The main managing structure of the Coalition is the Steering Council, which is composed of delegates from ten Northern organizations and three Amazonian organizations. The Steering Council meets at a minimum of four times a year, once in California, once in Washington,D.C. (the headquarters), and twice in Amazonian basin countries. Thus, Coalition members meet frequently to plan policies and mobilization strategies.

A Management Team composed of the Coordinator, vice-chair, secretary, and treasurer directs the administrative tasks of the Coalition. This team is located in the coordinating office, based in Washington,D.C. They are responsible for correspondence and communications to members, informing members of problems or policies in other Amazonian countries, and organizing all conferences and reunions between members. The Coordinating office sponsors Amazonian members to visit Washington, D.C. to speak with Northern NGO members, or to consult with the World Bank on an average of once a month. Thus, aside from formal quarterly and bi-annual meetings, the Coalition often meets with Amazonian members for specific program and policy initiatives either in Washington, D.C., or in their home states (Interview Melina Silverston 1996). For example, the Coalition sponsored Leonardo Viteri's trip to Washington, D.C. to participation in the 1996 Latin America Studies Association Meeting. This was followed by cocktail parties and brown bag lunch talks with Viteri to communicate his viewpoints on development in the Amazon. These formal and informal meetings, e-mail, fax, and telephone communications foster a high level of social capital, although not within local, or close, spaces, which in turn creates strong social networks.

II. History of the Coalition

The initiative to form the Coalition began in 1990 in Iquitos, Peru, during an international conference on "The Environment and Indigenous Peoples" sponsored by COICA. At this meeting, the conference participants determined that the biosphere was not only composed of flora and fauna, but also of human (indigenous) life. COICA and Northern NGOs subsequently made a commitment to coordinate discourse and policies "to further indigenous rights" (Declaration of the Mission 1995). The Coalition considers itself an umbrella of organizations, which "seeks to reinforce ties, communication and collaboration between U.S. and Amazonian peoples' organizations" (Declaration of the Mission 1995).

The Coalition began to form its mobilization strategies with its first conference, in 1993, entitled "Amazon Initiative: A Working Conference to Protect Indigenous Rights." This conference sought to "formalize" alliances between Northern and Amazonian organizations. The result was the identification of future goals. These goals are: 1) the defense of territories, 2) environmental protection, 3) human rights, and 4) economic and social development. Thus, the Coalition and COICA jointly formulated common ways of viewing the world and common long-term goals.

The coordination among Northern and Amazonian members strengthened in 1994, when the Coalition opened a coordinating office in Washington, D.C. Since then, the Coalition has distributed a monthly newsletter to its members and has strengthened fax and e-mail communications and travel among members.

In order to formalize its organizational structure, in May 1995 the Coalition sponsored a second conference entitled, "Partnership." This conference approved the Coalition's formal structure and outlined strategies and plans for 1995–1996 within the four working group areas. The Coalition's first year under the new, formal structure was 1996. Although the Coalition began in 1993, it took two years of organization and fundraising to arrive at its now high level of transnational organization. Following the "Partnership" conference, the Coalition sponsored two more conferences, one in June 1996 and one in May 1997. These conferences deepened the level of social connection and strategy coordination among Coalition members. The following analysis of issues and political strategies will elucidate the high level of coordination between indigenous members and Northern NGO members.

III. Issues and Political Strategies

The Defense of Territories and Resources Working Group

This working group focuses on issues such as oil development, Brazilian territorial issues, biodiversity, and multilateral lending institutions. It includes members from Northern NGOs, such as Rainforest Action Network (RAN), Oxfam America, and the Inter-American Foundation (IAF). The majority of members, though, are from Amazonian organizations from Ecuador, Brazil, Venezuela, Bolivia, Surinam, and from COICA and the Instituto Amazanga, an Amazonian research institute based in Ecuador. These members communicate and coordinate programs throughout the year.

During 1995 and 1996, the members focused on making Amazonian leaders aware of the environmental dangers of oil development in their territories. In November 1995, the Coalition and COICA sponsored a workshop on oil development in Lago Agrio, Ecuador, the northeastern region, which has been heavily contaminated by Texaco. Representatives from Peru, Bolivia, Venezuela, Colombia, and Ecuador spent two days in conference with the leaders of the Cofán peoples to learn their strategies and experiences with oil companies (Amazon Update #9 December 15, 1996). This conference led Peruvian officials to investigate the possibilities of a lawsuit in the United States against Shell Oil Company. It also fostered interaction and increased communication among indigenous leaders, INGO representatives, and academic researchers.

In March 1996, the working group helped facilitate the participation of sixty indigenous delegates from the Ecuadorian Amazon in a congressional hearing on the government's position in the cleanup of the Texaco area. In November 1996, the Coalition sent an international press release about the situation of the class-action lawsuit of Maria Aguinda et. al. v. Texaco, Inc., in which the Ecuadorian government did not support US jurisdiction in the case. After pressure from the Coalition, environmental groups, and the US State Department, the Ecuadorian government reconsidered its position, deciding to intervene on behalf of the plaintiffs in the case. The case is currently pending in the New York court system.

In May, Isauro Puente, President of the Ecuadorian Congressional Committee on the Environment, visited a Texaco shareholders' meeting, facilitated by the Coalition, and met with Washington D.C.-based INGO leaders. Thus, the Coalition improved dialogue among Northern based NGOs, multinational oil companies, and the indigenous communities.

In November 1996, RAN representative Shannon Wright visited Oxy Oil Company in Quito, Ecuador to discuss issues regarding the Siona and Secoya peoples. I met with Shannon Wright in the office of Acción Ecológica, an Ecuadorian INGO, and in the house of Juan Aulestia, a former consultant for COICA and the CONAIE. While I was meeting with Ms. Wright, three other indigenous leaders to whom she referred with familiarity were waiting to speak with her. She was meeting with other

INGO representatives in the Quito-area as well. Thus, the nodes of the network are very close, even though the distance between actors is great.

Aside from monitoring oil development in the Amazon, the Coalition is also involved in mining and deforestation issues. Two INGOs, Rainforest Action Network (RAN) and World Resources Institute (WRI), have been especially involved in negotiations between indigenous communities and private companies. In Guyana, WRI has been the advisor to the President on forest policy. In Suriname, RAN has aided indigenous leaders and private logging companies negotiate proposals for reforestation projects. In each case, these INGO members communicate with the main Coalition office in Washington D.C. to coordinate all policies and disseminate information about their activities.

This working group also focuses on funding and resources from multilateral development banks. One of the primary roles of the Coalition is to develop funding sources from the North that are not readily available to Amazonian indigenous groups. The Coalition often monitors World Bank activities and advises Bank officials in forming policies and projects in the Amazon. For example, the Coalition is monitoring and helping plan the World Bank Environmental Management and Technical Assistance Project, which is a $15 million program to develop regional environmental planning and grassroots projects in the Amazon. Moreover, the Bank Information Center (BIC) and Red Bancos gave a one-day workshop to CONAIE leaders in Ecuador on multilateral bank funding and indigenous peoples, sponsored and organized by the Coalition. Finally, BIC and Red Bancos members visited Lago Agrio, Shushufindi, and Coca, Ecuadorian Amazon areas affected by oil development, after their workshop to analyze the World Bank environmental projects being implemented in these regions (The Coalition Annual Meeting Report 1996:29–30).

Sustainable Communities Working Group

This working group is composed of indigenous and non-indigenous INGO members. Its goal is to develop long term strategies of economic and social development, while protecting "the future integrity of their communities" (The Coalition Annual Report 1996: 33). A leader in this working group is Leonardo Viteri, an Ecuadorian Quichua, who is director of the Amazanga Institute, a private institute in the Ecuadorian Amazon dedicated to creating sustainable development projects in the Amazon. The main purpose of this group is to create a common concept of sustainable development among the communities and communicate this concept to all members. The working group members from the Amazon and from the U.S. and Europe meet twice a year in Washington D.C. to analyze Coalition activities and monitor the progress of projects underway.

Collective Rights and International Policy Working Group

This working group is dedicated to the international rights of indigenous peoples and focuses on communications with international organizations. This group is also composed of indigenous and non-indigenous members. It primarily monitors the policies developed by international organizations and analyzes their potential impacts on indigenous communities. Moreover, this group develops and introduces new policies for indigenous peoples in international organizations.

The working group sent a Draft Declaration of the Rights of Indigenous Peoples of the OAS to other indigenous organizations to coordinate input and changes. They also sent letters advocating the rights of indigenous peoples to all of the leaders of states in Latin America and the World Bank. In May and June 1996, they sponsored two U.S. Congressional briefings on oil development in Ecuador. In June 1996, the working group hosted a meeting in the World Bank to discuss the role of the NGO-Liaison officers of the bank.

Aside from these activities, this group also sponsors visits from indigenous leaders to Washington D.C. to present their cases to the World Bank and INGO leaders. In October 1995, Kayapo Xikrin, from Brazil, visited Washington D.C. and in April 1996, Sergio Tembe from Brazil spoke with World Bank and U.S. Congressional members about the situation of indigenous peoples in the Brazilian Amazon. These visits were coordinated with COICA activities in Brazil. Thus, the Coalition has bridged the gap between indigenous leaders and international organizations by creating nodes of direct communication among the parties. (The Coalition Annual Report 1996: 35).

IV. The Coalition as a Transnational Social Movement

The Coalition for Amazonian Peoples and their Environment is a transnational social movement because it has sustained levels of collective action, shared visions of the world, and close levels of networks among its members. The Coalition functions as coordinator between Northern INGO members and indigenous peoples. Its activities are purposely based on the international level to improve awareness and resources for its sister movement, COICA. Thus, both TSMOs work together to coordinate broader, international support for Amazonian indigenous peoples.

Although members of the Coalition are not all indigenous and do not all live in the same region, they overcome common social network boundaries through frequent visits, conferences, e-mail, and fax. Members of the Coalition, when visiting Amazonian countries, often stay in the houses of indigenous members. The members of working groups often become friends and send personal messages via the Internet. This was witnessed personally in various conferences held in Quito when U.S.-based INGO members would often converse with indigenous members about their families and other private matters. Thus, the Coalition has created an international space for people of similar visions of the world to coordinate activities and policies in the form of a transnational social movement.

CONCLUSION

COICA and the Coalition are two examples of transnational social movements, which are affecting international and national policies for indigenous peoples. Both cases fit the definition of transnational social movements employed in this project, which is "sustained interactions with opponents based on the claims of connected networks of challengers organized on the basis of collective interests and values across national boundaries" (Tarrow 1998:414). COICA and the Coalition are movements, which are integrated in several societies with shared visions of the world and sustained interaction throughout a number of cases and events. Therefore, they share depth, or collective identities and common purposes and breadth, or high levels of communication and networks.

COICA and the Coalition have coordinated efforts on issues such as the environment, including flora, fauna, rivers, territory, and human life, petroleum development, mineral development, wood industry, human rights, intellectual property, and border disputes. Their opponents are members of the international community, such as MNCs or IGOs, and institutions of their member-states. Their values are based around preserving the environment of the Amazon and the lives and customs of indigenous peoples. These values are internalized through common identities. While the identities of Coalition members are those of ecology and indigenous lifestyles, the identity of COICA is that of a community of Amazonian indigenous peoples. Both shared views of the world aid in bonding these movements and making them sustained, rather than fleeting. Finally, COICA and the Coalition share communication networks. These networks are operationalized through the Internet, telephone, fax, easy means of travel, and constant visits to member-states. In the case of COICA, members from various states work together to coordinate policies in Quito, Ecuador. In the case of the Coalition, members coordinate via common committees, or working groups, which meet at various times each year. These close networks not only reinforce group organization and mobilization strategies, but also aid in strengthening and maintaining shared identities among members.

While the mobilization and organization strategies of these TSMOs are active and sustained, their outcomes are less impressive. The outcomes of the issue-events of COICA and the Coalition are primarily evident on the transnational level in the form of information dissemination, increased awareness, international conferences, and change in the policy of an international organization. However, in the six COICA issue-events studied and the three Coalition events very few led to sanctioning an international or domestic actor.

In the case of COICA, two Brazilian gold miners were arrested for killing indigenous peoples. Furthermore, a governmental investigation on a national level was conducted on the impacts of mineral extraction in the Brazilian Amazon on the indigenous peoples in those areas. Also, in the case of the border dispute between Ecuador and Peru, the COICA conference and campaign prompted an OAS investigation of the impacts of the conflict on indigenous communities and an OAS-sponsored conference between the Peruvian and Ecuadorian indigenous communities to share information and strategies to prevent further conflict in their regions. Finally, in the case of petroleum development, COICA has been successful in educating their fellow member organizations about sustainable development programs and forms of negotiation to implement them with oil company representatives. While COICA has not played an active role in shaping the outcomes of negotiations, it has provided technical and negotiation consultation on behalf of its member-state representatives. As noted in Chapter 4, the activism of Amazonian indigenous peoples with regard to petroleum development has changed seismic testing and extraction policies, as well as prompted incremental funding for social programs. Thus, COICA was only successful in one case, the case of Brazilian Amazonian peoples, in attaining a sanction against gold miners. In the other cases, COICA was successful in changing international organization or MNC policies.

In the case of the Peruvian Ashaninkas, free trade in the Americas, and the Ayahuasca campaigns, COICA was only marginally successful in affecting policy change. Campaigns in these cases served to increase a form of international awareness and disseminate information. However, no concrete policy changes or investigations into the issue-area were observed.

In the case of the Coalition, the issue-area of "Territories and Resources" was much more successful in obtaining policy change and concrete outcomes from their transnational mobilization strategies. Through the Coalition-sponsored workshop between Ecuadorian and Peruvian indigenous communities affected by oil development, both communities filed lawsuits against Texaco and Shell oil companies in the New York court system. Following a U.S. Congressional hearing on U.S. overseas oil companies and their activities and Coalition-NGO member concerns, Texaco oil company accepted a multi-million dollar cleanup plan for the Ecuadorian Amazon following twenty years of petroleum extraction in the Northern-Amazonian region. Finally, the Coalition secured a $15 million project on Environmental Management and Technical Assistance in the Amazon from the World Bank. Also, in the case of "Collective Rights and International Politics," the Coalition prepared the Declaration of Rights of Indigenous Peoples for the OAS, which was later accepted as an official OAS document. Thus, the transnational mobilization strategies of the Coalition have been successful in the area of sanctioning with the case of oil companies and the Texaco cleanup plan, and in the case of policy development and change in the case of the World Bank and the OAS.

There are two implications of the analysis of outcomes of this chapter. First, TSMOs get results on both domestic and transnational levels. This shows that the mobilization strategies utilized are geared toward multiple levels. However, in the cases presented in this chapter, the outcomes were found to be of a primarily transnational nature via international organizations or MNCs. Second, certain issues seem to be more likely to capture international attention and reaction. As described in Chapter 2, I argue that states are bound to both their international as well as national environments in the case of transnational contentious politics. In the case of the environment and indigenous peoples, it has been in the interest of Amazonian states to defer their sovereignty to private actors. This implies that the issue-area has been internationalized to the point that the state has lost some autonomy over the issue. Thus, in the case of the environment and sustainable development, and to a lesser extent, human rights, private actors such as COICA and the Coalition have been effective not only in changing transnational policy, but also in affecting domestic policy outcomes. Moreover, the diffusion of information and ideas contributes to changes in the international norms of transnational and domestic actors.

Finally, transnational social movements are still linked to the domestic social movement organizations of member-states. The success of COICA and the Coalition is, in part, based on the effective mobilization and organization of their domestic bases. For example, COICA is composed of sustained, domestic social movement organizations from Amazonian countries. While the press releases and transnational communications function on the level of transnational leaders and international private actors, mobilization, strategy implementation, and outcomes depend greatly on a TSMO that has strong grassroots bases.

However, the impacts of transnational social movement organizations are not always positive for national development of a coherent social movement. In the case of Ecuador, the transnationalization of the Amazon has caused tensions within the Amazon and separated it from its Sierra neighbors. Wealthier Amazonian organizations are looked upon as taking funds from smaller, less wealthy Amazonian neighbors. The Sierra peoples, due to their lack of transnational mobilization, have organized themselves through other, state-linked structures. Thus, the ability to change national policy for all indigenous peoples is impaired due to the division among movements.

NOTES

[1] Coordinadora de Organizaciones Indígenas de la Cuenca Amazónica, or Coordinator of Indigenous Organizations in the Amazon Basin

[2] I will utilize the term "Coalition" to refer to the Coalition of Amazonian Peoples and their Environment.

[3] The term "Northern" in this context refers to non-Latin American countries, primarily developed countries. The Coalition and COICA refer to these members as "Northern" in their discourse.

[4] The Coalition defines indigenous and traditional peoples as "people who live in harmony with the ecosystem, including rubber tapers, tribal peoples and indigenous peoples." It defines support organizations as "those human rights, environmental and support groups that work directly with indigenous and traditional peoples (Annual Report 1996:24).

CHAPTER SIX

Analysis and Conclusions

INTRODUCTION

MANY SCHOLARS HAVE EMPLOYED THE TERM "GLOBALIZATION" to encompass the changing pattern of world events, including growth in telecommunications, technology, travel, and market forces. However, this dynamic panoply of developments has also impacted the ways in which people organize, mobilize, and seek to change policy outcomes. During the 1960s and 1970s in Latin America, the organization and mobilization of many domestic social movements was stifled due to military dictatorships that governed civil life. While the 1980s witnessed an unprecedented democratization of the region, the most under-represented peoples, indigenous peoples, continued to experience a lack of fora to express their needs and demands. Therefore, the 1980s also experienced a backlash of social organization and mobilization, which was not based on the state level, but rather on the international level. As Alison Brysk states, the Latin American Indian rights movement was "born transnational" (Brysk 1994: 35).

The previous two chapters analyze forms of transnational contentious collective action through empirical evidence of case studies. As Kathryn Sikkink and Margaret Keck suggest, at this point in the theoretical development of transnational processes of collective action, we are "better served by examining the linkage processes than by trying to draw the outlines of the new patterns these linkages may be producing" (1998: 237). Chapters Four and Five elucidated these complex, transnational linkage processes, how they function, and their effectiveness and outcomes.

The literatures of social movement theory, international political economy, transnational relations, and ethnic conflict were weaved together to create the model on which this project is based.

SOCIAL MOVEMENT THEORY

Social movement theory best examines the processes of domestic contentious collective action. Although the case of the Amazonian indigenous rights movement is not domestic in nature, much of the literature is applicable to the transnationalization of the process. Transnational contentious collective action, however, diverges slightly on five levels: 1) political opportunity structures, 2) social networks, 3) identity, 4) framing, and 5) outcomes. Each of these levels of analysis expands once on the transnational level, yet still may be considered aspects of social movements.

While transnational advocacy networks are not social movements due to their lack of sustained mobilizing actions, transnational social movements are a social movement form. However, transnational social movements do not respond mainly to domestic political opportunity structures, such as change in government, or political institutions.[1] Transnational social movements may benefit from change in national political institutions, but tend to form via new venues created in the international realm, such as opportunities in international organizations. Therefore, there are new and varied levels of political opportunity structures.

Social networks have been cited as key factors in the formation of movement organizations and in the sustainability of mobilization.[2] Transnational social movement organizations transport these social ties to a more distant, yet still effective, level. As discussed in Chapter Five, social networks are maintained transnationally through the shared commonalities and visions of peoples. These networks are also stimulated through frequent meetings and communications. As the telecommunications technology allows individuals to breakdown spatial barriers, the inability of movement participants to develop social ties dissipates. Thus, the once town-based social networks that were vital to movement organization and mobilization are now being augmented to include the broader, global village.

Included in the discussion of social networks is identity. Traditionally, identity forms the common vision of a movement and defines the frames in which it is based. However, the existence of common identities on a transnational level has been a much-debated point. Identities may now be being "born" on a transnational level and thus, created from a top-down model instead of the traditional bottom-up approach. Therefore, transnational networks are forming groups of people with common identities that cross state borders. Paul Wapner (1996), in his analysis of world environmental activism, refers to this concept as a global civil society in which certain values are recognized and acted upon on an international level.

The framing process is the way in which movements define themselves to attract new participants and to counter their adversaries. Framing includes elements of culture, strategy, and the role of the media on both a domestic and transnational level (McAdam, McCarthy, and Zald 1996: 19). The most important issue for transnational social movements in the framing process, based on this research and previous, is the master frame. The master frame functions as the global idea, which acts as the catalyst for the movement. Within this master frame, specific, culturally oriented smaller frames may exist to attract new members and identify culturally specific targets. This signals a mesh of local cultures and transnational ideas, or the transnationalization of "locality."

Finally, outcomes may vary in transnational social movements and domestic social movements. While we would expect outcomes on a national level for domestic social movements, transnational social movements can expect outcomes on transnational levels, such as in international organizations, MNCs, INGOs, as well as on the domestic level. Moreover, as demonstrated through the case studies in this project, many times, regional and local outcomes are predominant in the transnational social movement process because the state is either not involved or not responsive to the mobilization (Chapter Four and Five). Thus, an analysis that includes only outcomes on the state level would be missing many other outcome possibilities.

THE PUBLIC/PRIVATE DEBATE

Throughout this analysis, it has been argued that non-state actors are private actors, which possess authority in the international system (Chapter Two).[3] This argument assumes that the state is not the sole force of authority in the international system and that, in fact, other non-state, private actors may take on the role of public actors in certain circumstances. Susan Strange supports this argument in her analysis of The Retreat of the State, in which she argues that there is a diffusion of authority in the international system. This diffusion, due to factors of the world market and increased technology and communication, has diminished the power of the state as a completely sovereign actor. Two main foci of her study are MNCs and society. Strange examines the ways in which these actors obtain and diffuse authority, and impact outcomes. This research project develops Strange's concepts by empirically examining the interplay of authority among private actors and the role of the state in this situation.

Strange argues that MNCs have multiple loyalties, including interests that go beyond the purely economic, profit-making realm. She argues that firms have a "political nature of corporate policymaking and diplomacy." Moreover, they have the power "to change society and politics as much as business..." (1996: 186). As discussed in Chapter Two and Chapter Four, this project views MNCs as not solely profit-oriented actors. Therefore, their authority may be analyzed through the lens of societal and political change, as well as economic. In the case of the Ecuadorian Amazon, MNCs have acted as public advocates for health, education, and community development projects. In some instances, oil company executives admitted that they assume the state does not even exist (Chapter Four). Thus, their private authority is manifested on a very public, societal level.

Moreover, Strange argues that international political economists need to further examine the impacts of the market and market actors on the societal level (1996: 188). This type of analysis includes the study of the societal level through social movement theory and the relationship between social movements and transnational actors. In the Amazonian case, societal actors have merged with transnational actors who include not only INGOs, but also MNCs, to form transnational advocacy networks and in some cases, transnational social movement organizations, all of which have impacted both the societal and the transnational actors in terms of organization, mobilization strategies, negotiation procedures, and policy change and outcomes. This transnational bridge between private actors on international and domestic levels circumvents state authority and implements a new policy formation and outcome process.

In cases in which the issue-area is highly internationally oriented, such as the environment or human rights, the state is placed in a position of negotiation with actors (Chapter Two). The state, in such cases, must negotiate with all parties, including private, transnational actors, which have stakes in the policy implementation process within the state. While the state does not completely lose its authority, its complete autonomy to implement policy is diminished. In the case of the Ecuadorian Amazon, the state played a minimal role in circumstances that were highly politicized by private, transnational actors, such as the Texaco oil case and the Cofánes. However, in 1972, when there were few transnational actors to combat, the state was not forced to negotiate its policies. Thus, one of the outcomes of transnational contentious collective action is that it has created international themes, or issue areas, which are globally recognized, accepted, and acted upon.

The accessibility of international resources, such as funding from international donor agencies or international non-governmental organizations, combined with the facility of international communication and travel has broadened the scope of social movement organization to the transnational level. However, this change in organization not only influences the societal level, but rather affects the role of the state and non-state actors in the international system. While globalization may not be occurring in the strong sense of the definition in all sectors of the international system, a modern diffusion of power in the system is being observed based on the ability of resource-poor Amazonian actors to mobilize and influence policy change on various levels.

THE EMERGENCE OF TRANSNATIONAL CONTENTIOUS COLLECTIVE ACTION

The first hypothesis of this project proposes that transnational contentious collective action emerges under the following conditions: a) when there are constraints and blockages in the domestic system; b) when there are international political opportunities and mobilizing structures which create openings for resource-poor actors; and c) when the interests of domestic groups and transnational actors complement each other. This hypothesis addresses the expansion of political opportunity structures and resources for social movements beyond the domestic sphere. In order to analyze these factors, an historical analysis of the factors that caused blockage and created new political opportunities is necessary. Thus, unlike much of the literature on "new" social movements, which focuses on modern events and movements, this study requires historical analysis to understand the varied influences on transnational contentious collective action.

An overriding element of the development of both the Amazonian social movement and the transnational advocacy networks of the Ecuadorian Amazon is the historical blockages, which these groups have experienced to their organization and mobilization. As discussed in Chapter Three, Amazonian leaders initiated the transnational Amazonian indigenous rights movement during the time period of military dictatorships in Latin America. Also during that same time, many MNCs were investing in Latin American subsidiaries for the development of timber, rubber, and oil industries. This influx of industry in the Amazon, a region, which had been largely unpopulated by non-indigenous peoples, affected not only the economy of Amazonian countries, but the social organization of its peoples.

In the late 1970s and early 1980s, Amazonian countries began to democratize and create new constitutions, which included the largely excluded indigenous populations. However, these apparent openings in the national political structure did not impact indigenous peoples in the Amazon. Being geographically detached from the main centers of their countries, many Amazonian peoples did not experience a change in political representation. As one Shuar commented to me, "I am Shuar. It truly does not matter if I am Ecuadorian or Peruvian because I have never felt a governmental presence in my life" (Interview May 13, 1998). Moreover, governmental institutions in Amazonian countries did not change to augment representation of their indigenous populations. Rather, some, such as Colombia and Brazil, recognized indigenous populations in their national constitutions without providing new institutions to represent them.[4] In the case of Ecuador, the literacy qualification to vote was removed, but political education and information was not provided to aid indigenous peoples in the new process. Thus, Amazonian peoples remained largely excluded from national political systems.

In the case of Ecuador, the Amazon remained a separate region not only in informal interactions within the country, but legally. The Amazon was treated as a special, under-developed region of the country in national governmental documents and policies. Until the 1994 founding of the Secretary of Indigenous Affairs under the presidential ministry, there were no formal political institutions representing indigenous peoples. In governmental documents prior to the 1960s, many do not even acknowledge that populations existed in that part of the country. During the military dictatorship of General Rodriguez Lara, oil development was at its all-time high in the country and without consultation with the indigenous populations. Thus, pre-democratic Ecuador did not provide the political opportunity structures necessary for the formation of a domestic social movement.

With the transition to democracy in 1979, indigenous peoples were more able to form political organizations. However, their political representation did not change. These populations remained almost wholly excluded from the national political system. The first national political representative of Amazonian peoples in Ecuador was appointed in 1996 by now-exiled ex-president, Abdala Bucaram. This Shuar leader, Raphael Pandam, lost his ministerial position during the presidential coup of February 1997 and was later accused of embezzling government funds and accepting bribes. Thus, post-democratic openings were very few in the national political system.[5]

Although domestic openings were lacking for Amazonian indigenous peoples, the 1960s brought a new surge in social and political organization for them. During this period, missionaries founded political and social organizations and anthropologists set the foundations for later international meetings. These initial contacts were the foundations for transnational advocacy networks throughout the region. They provided information from outside the Amazon and offered education to largely uneducated populations. Thus, openings began to form for the creation of transnational nodes of communication and organization.

During the 1970s and 1980s, various international conferences were sponsored for indigenous peoples. These conferences inspired further integration of the Amazonian indigenous movement and also, allowed Amazonian peoples to share common concerns and create common bonds of identity. These common bonds of identity and social networks grew into COICA by 1984. With the foundation of this transnational social movement organization, international organizations began to provide resources for organization and mobilization. Thus, the World Bank and INGOs, such as Oxfam America and the Inter-American Foundation, provided these once resource-poor actors with new political opportunities and new mobilizing structures completely outside of the realm of the state.

In the Ecuadorian case, indigenous peoples have found various openings in the international system for their mobilization. The Cofánes utilized resources from the Natural Resources Defense Fund (NRDC) to file a lawsuit again Texaco in New York. Rainforest Action Network (RAN), Acción Ecológica, and National Wildlife Federation (NWF) sponsored meetings to education the Cofánes about oil development in their area and to link them through transnational networks with other INGOs involved in similar issue-areas. Moreover, the Cofánes, through the leadership of their half North American—half Cofán leader, Randy Borman, have established an eco-tourism project in their sector of the Amazon. Thus, transnational actors provided resources sufficient to spur increased mobilization and participation in the transnational advocacy network.

In the case of the Organization of Indigenous Peoples of Pastaza (OPIP), transnational actors provided the political opportunity structures and resources needed to counter oil development in their southern-Amazonian sector. While initially aided by INGOs such as RAN, Oxfam America, and IBIS-Denmark, OPIP later joined forces with ARCO Oil Company to negotiate directly and participate in policymaking in their region. One direct example of resources given to OPIP was a $20,000 grant awarded to them by RAN to sponsor their 1992 march from the lowlands to the highland capital of Quito. Moreover, direct resources have been provided by ARCO in the form of medical clinics, potable water, cattle selling, and investment in artisanship projects (Chapter Four). These transnational resources have provided openings that were non-existent via the state.

Other forms of political opportunities can also be observed in Ecuador. The INGOs involved in the transnational advocacy network provide ideological support in the sense that they work on issue-areas of common interest globally. They also provide resources to create newsletters and e-mail communication. All of the Amazonian indigenous confederations have at least fax communication that was sponsored by transnational funding. For instance, the OPIP office has three telephone lines (a rarity for any organization in Ecuador), e-mail, and two fax machines all provided by various INGO funds. Finally, MNCs and INGOs provide information resources to these organizations in the form of technical consultation. Thus, the resources, which contribute to political opportunities, are in diverse forms ranging from information and discourse to direct project funding.

The mobilizing structures of transnational advocacy networks and transnational social movements differ due to their sustainability. In the case of transnational advocacy networks, mobilization is episodic and based upon an issue area. However, mobilization in transnational social movements is not fleeting, but sustained and based upon a common agenda of action over a long time period. In Ecuador, for instance, the transnational advocacy networks of the indigenous confederations are extensive, yet episodic and based upon new issue areas, such as oil development in specific Amazonian blocks or new agricultural programs. Thus, indigenous confederations connect and disconnect with the nodes of the networks when issue areas of interest to them arise. However, COICA and the Coalition are transnational social movement organizations that are based upon a common identity and have long-term programmatic goals. These groups maintain their mobilization via forms of telecommunications and travel. Although their issues may change and their strategies may be diverse, their common visions and forms of organization and mobilization do not rise and fall based on single issues.

Moreover, because transnational advocacy networks tend to be episodic in mobilization, their allies and targets within the networks may change. This lack of consistency within the nodes of the network can cause a breakdown among indigenous movements. One such case is in the Northern Ecuadorian Amazon in which the Quichua and the Siona and Secoya Indians cannot agree on policies in the region that they share. Each has chosen different actors in the network with whom to work. Thus, the Quichua Indians prefer negotiations with Occidental, while the Siona and Secoya Indians are mobilizing with Acción Ecológica and RAN against oil development in this region. As observed through these particular cases, transnational networks may augment political opportunity structures, while at the same time decrease sustainability of mobilization and unity among local and regional movements (Chapter Four).

IMPACTS ON ORGANIZATION, STRATEGIES, AND EFFECTIVENESS

Hypothesis two focuses on the change in strategies and collective activities when a movement joins transnational advocacy network nodes. Participation in this web of transnational communications and resources transforms mobilization strategies and collective action activities such that domestic strategies incorporate transnational actors or utilize not previously acquired transnational resources, and collective activity takes place on multiple levels, meaning local, national, and international. Moreover, this section of the project argued that policy outcomes would be observed on both domestic and transnational levels. The results from this research do indicate that organization and mobilization strategies are altered on the transnational level such that organization is expanded and professionalized and mobilization is broadened to include strategies that encompass not only domestic, but also transnational actors.

Organization

On an organizational level, there are five dimensions of change that can be extracted from these case studies: a) professionalism of the movements; b) division between the movement leadership and participants; c) division among local movements that prevents national movement cohesion; d) an upward form of organizational development as opposed to a lateral, national form of organization, and e) increased commonalities between domestic and transnational actors. In the case of transnational social movements, the division between the transnational leaders and those in the grassroots operations may be even greater. Furthermore, the essence of a transnational social movement organization is the just that: transnational, implying that a national movement is not in their interest to form. Finally, the commonalities among domestic and transnational actors are far stronger in a transnational social movement than in transnational advocacy networks due to the sustained mobilization and the common identity shared among members. Thus, while organizational change characteristics can be generalized, there are levels of difference between transnational advocacy networks and transnational social movements.

With regard to transnational advocacy networks, the case studies in this project suggest that links with transnational actors professionalize the movements, decreasing their reliance on aggressive, violent tactics. Sidney Tarrow and David Meyer note the professionalization of European movements, such as central offices, networks of activists, and complex, technical campaigns (1998:17). However, transnational advocacy networks transport their professional tactics from Northern-based activists to Southern-based activists. Therefore, even Amazonian movements, which until recently may not have utilized telephones, are now hooked up to the internet and sending e-mails to Northern colleagues.

I have found that the organizations that have higher levels of professionalism tend to be more successful in realizing their demands. For example, in the case of the Siona and the Secoya, their organization is relatively new. They do not have technical support teams, nor do they have a long history of participation in transnational networks. However, their Quichua neighbors (FOISE) have been long-time participants in transnational networks and have sent leaders to seminars on petroleum production in order to better inform their organization in negotiations with oil companies. Moreover, FOISE (the Quichua organization) has a branch office in Quito to meet with government, transnational, and oil company officials. The Siona and Secoya have not reached this level of professionalism at this point. In spite of the fact that these two groups are the least professionalized of the four case studies, the Quichua have managed to negotiate directly with Occidental to implement policy change in their town. The Siona and Secoya, while successful in diffusing information about their cause and mobilizing tactics with other INGOs, have not been able to change policy outcomes in their towns.

The third most professional organization is that of the Cofánes. Under the leadership of Randy Borman, they participated in and hosted conferences in South America about oil development in the rainforest and developed eco-tourism projects to alert people of the dangers of petroleum development in the Amazon. Moreover, through international financing via INGOs, they have filed a lawsuit against Texaco for the environmental degradation of their region. Unlike the Quichua, Siona, and Secoya, the Cofánes have written books on their situation, utilized journals and newsletters, and can be reached via e-mail. Their members have traveled to Washington, D.C. to testify in the U.S. Congress and they too have a central office in Ecuador. The Cofánes successfully lobbied Texaco and the Ecuadorian government, through transnational advocacy networks, to initiate a $1.2 billion clean-up plan in their region.

Finally, OPIP, the Quichua Indians of Pastaza, is the most professionalized of the organizations studied in Chapter Four. Their leaders have been sent to graduate study programs on petroleum development and industry. They established, through the Amazonga Institute, a sustainable development project, a research institute, and have formed a technical support staff, which consults on cases and advises other Amazonian groups with regard to oil development in their regions. OPIP has successfully gained land grants from the Ecuadorian government, as well as policy changes within ARCO, such as being included in their policy-making institutions.

While this level of professionalism advances the bargaining and negotiating ability of the organization with other transnational actors, such as INGOs and MNCs, and the government, it also hinders cohesion within the group. In an interview with Leonardo Viteri, an OPIP leader and director of the Amazonga Institute, he noted that there is a division that occurs between members and leaders, particularly when the leaders travel outside the country and bring back new discourse and ideas (Interview March 7, 1997). While leaders seek to integrate participants and diffuse new ideas to them, their visions tend to change once they leave the Amazon. This can cause a weakening of the grassroots mobilization of the organization and a strengthening of transnational mobilization. Organizations such as OPIP that are highly transnationalized are challenged, as expressed by their leadership, to unite participants under local frames with international themes.

As groups compete for international funding, coherence on a national level also decreases. International funding institutions, such as the World Bank and the Inter-American Development Bank, offer funds for grassroots, sustainable development projects, which attract social movements. Therefore, social movement organizations connect with other transnational actors in the network to apply for and influence funding for their region and project. This creates competition among social movement organizations within the same region or country. It also creates the potential for divions at the local level. In the case of Ecuador, this occurred between the Quichuas and the Siona and Secoya peoples in the Northern Amazon. Both groups are acting via international advocacy networks as opposed to their regional organization of the Amazon, CONFENIAE. They are competing for funding and projects.

On a broader scale, the national indigenous organization, CONAIE, has also experienced problems due to competition among regions and localities. Although the national organization has increased in mobilization throughout the 1990s, it lacks coherency between Sierra and Amazonian groups. More specifically, in January 1997, there were protests in front of its Quito office against an OPIP, Quichua leader from becoming president. Not only did Sierra peoples protest, but also other Amazonian organiza-

tions joined in protest. This signifies a division within the national movement, I argue, not solely based on identity, but also based on links with
transnational actors. OPIP, being a highly transnationalized actor, has been
very successful in obtaining funds for mobilization activities, while other
Sierra and Amazonian organizations have not been as successful.

This lack of national organization and mobilization suggests an
upward form of organization as opposed to a lateral, national form of
organization in which groups unite first on local, then regional, then
national levels. As Alison Brysk (1993,1994) argues, the danger of transnational organization and mobilization is that groups do not unite on a
national level. This creates disjunctures in policy-making at the national
level with state officials because state officials are unsure who is the "true"
representative of the group. As demonstrated by the Quichua and Siona
and Secoya cases, there is not just one, single voice echoed from the
Amazon, nor from the Sierra. Therefore, we observe a circumvention of the
state level of organization, directly to the transnational level. While this
form of organization has been successful due to state blockages, it could
also be the deterrent for domestic social movements.

The increasing convenience of organization on a transnational level,
due to telecommunication and travel, has strengthened the role of transnational social movement organizations, in this case, COICA and the
Coalition. These organizations have benefited from state blockages and
captured a space for Amazonian peoples. Thus, the increase in organization
and mobilization at the transnational level also signals an increase in
authority for transnational social movement organizations, which have
taken the place in many cases, of the national social movement.

The last characteristic of change in organization is commonalities.
As commonalities between transnational actors and domestic actors
increase in the transnational advocacy network, so too does the level of
transnational mobilization. These commonalities include ideas, discourse,
framing, projects, and identity. As noted in Chapters Three and Four,
Amazonian peoples did not begin their movements as environmentalists.
Rather, they linked with other nodes of the environmental advocacy network and incorporated their frames into Amazonian frames already in
place. As this interaction increased, projects between actors also developed,
which further integrated them. The final outcome is a tightly woven network in which an identity is shared. As this identity becomes deeper and
the relationships grow stronger, a transnational social movement organization can form.

In the case of OPIP, their organization and mobilization began with
small, short-lived issue-oriented events. However, as their involvement in

the transnational advocacy network increased, their mobilization strategies extended to longer time periods with common projects as the outcomes. For instance, IBIS-Denmark and the Inter-American Foundation coordinate projects in Pastaza, which span two-and three-year time periods. This is an advance in sustainability from their 1992 protest march to Quito from Pastaza with the help of a grant from RAN. Thus, augmenting commonalities causes an increase in transnational collective activity.

Mobilization

Hypothesis Two also suggests that collective activity will expand to national and transnational levels from local levels as transnational collective activity builds. While a minor expansion of collective activity was observed on a national level, far more expansion of collective activity was observed on the transnational level. The state was the target of mobilization in most of the cases of transnational advocacy networks, but not the sole target. Rather, these issues lend themselves to transnational collective action due to the involvement of transnational actors in the policymaking processes. Thus, multiple targets of mobilization are noted, such as IGOs, MNCs, and/or the state.

Transnational advocacy networks aided the domestic movements of the Amazon to gain a voice within national politics. Since the 1990 uprising, it is now a common occurrence for Amazonian peoples to march in Quito, the capital, hundreds of miles from their towns. Moreover, CONAIE, the national indigenous organization, has incorporated Amazonian peoples' demands in their charter and speaks on their behalf. Ex-president Abdala Bucaram recognized the Amazonian ethnic identity nationally by appointing a Shuar Indian as Minister of Ethnic Affairs. Finally, in the case of the Cofánes, they utilized INGOs to organize protests and hearings in the U.S. Congress to influence the Ecuadorian state. They were ultimately successful in obtaining an environmental clean-up project in their region.

On a larger scale, the inclusion of transnational actors in collective activity has broadened mobilization across borders. For instance, in 1993, the Coalition and COICA organized a boycott of Texaco in the United States. In 1996, a protest was staged on behalf of the Siona and Secoya Indians (with Siona and Secoya Indians present) against Occidental at their headquarters in California. Moreover, non-state, international organizations or MNC policies are targets of mobilization. For instance, COICA members targeted their mobilization against timber companies in Guyana, oil companies in Peru and Ecuador, and rubber and gold industries in Brazil and Venezuela. Thus, non-state actors are targets of mobilization, which changes the strategies utilized and expands the transnational scope of collective activity.

Effectiveness

Sikkink and Keck suggest five stages of effectiveness for transnational advocacy networks. This project analyzes these five stages and includes variations in the five stages based upon differences of level of intensity of mobilization, such as transnational advocacy network or transnational social movement. The five stages of effectiveness are: 1) framing debates and getting issues on the agenda; 2) encouraging discursive commitments; 3) causing procedural change at the international and domestic level; 4) affecting policy; and 5) influencing behavior changes in target actors (Keck and Sikkink 1998: 201).

These cases suggest that transnational social movement organizations tend to be more effective in the areas of framing debates and encouraging discursive commitments, yet unlike the Keck and Sikkink volume, this study finds differences of effectiveness between transnational advocacy networks and transnational social movements on multiple levels. TSMOs guide the frames used by transnational advocacy networks. In the Amazonian case, both transnational advocacy networks and transnational social movements have been effective in the other three levels, yet with varying results. The Ecuadorian transnational advocacy networks, due to the strength in their local mobilization, were much more effective than transnational social movements in results on the local, regional, or domestic level. Moreover, transnational social movement organizations aided in this mobilization by providing the international discourse, resources, and pressure upon transnational and state actors to cause effective outcomes. However, the domestic actors of the transnational advocacy networks were the key players in the policymaking and implementation processes.

With regard to the framing of the Amazonian transnational social movement, this process began with initial meetings among non-indigenous and indigenous members in the late 1960s and throughout the 1970s and 1980s. The combination of environmental activists, anthropologists, and to a lesser extent, missionaries, created the common vision and frame that encompasses the larger movement. Thus, COICA and the Coalition envision and portray the Amazon as an integral part of the world environment, including indigenous peoples as the caretakers and holders of knowledge of this area. This master frame forms the foundation of the movement. Within this frame, the indigenous identity from the Amazon supports social networks, a common vision (or, Tarrow's version of "social capital"), and sustains organization and mobilization.

Transnational advocacy networks, as shown in the Ecuadorian case studies, utilize this umbrella of the master frame incorporates local symbols and traditions. For example, Quichua words, such as PachaMama (Mother Earth) are included in newsletters and propaganda from Ecuador to encourage sustained mobilization. Moreover, symbols such as Inti (the Incan sun) or the rainbow are included in Ecuadorian transnational advocacy networks as signals to the people. Thus, the general frame is set by the transnational social movement, which has already created the international space and discourse. Then, this discourse is adapted to fit local customs and cultures.

Transnational social movement organizations, as suggested by these cases and those by Paul Wapner (1996), are stronger in creating discussion among actors, while transnational advocacy networks are stronger in sustaining and implementing further discussions or negotiations. For example, the Coalition organized a conference in 1995 among Amazonian peoples to learn about oil development in the rainforest. Conference participants included state officials, private petroleum consultants, oil companies, activists, and indigenous peoples. This meeting furthered the discussion process between indigenous confederations, particularly in Ecuador and Peru, and oil companies. One result of this conference was negotiations between ARCO and OPIP and further deliberations between Texaco and the Cofánes. Thus, the transnational social movement organization created the discursive element and the transnational advocacy network participants utilized this space for their individual issue areas and regions.

Procedural change, although aided by the international space created by transnational social movement organizations was highly influenced by the mobilization of transnational advocacy networks. These actors, unsatisfied with the current state of procedure within negotiations of MNCs, the state, and INGOs , utilized transnational resources and discourse to encourage change. This procedural change was noted in the mobilization of OPIP, FOISE, and the Cofánes, in which oil companies and INGOs changed their procedures to include feedback and observations of indigenous peoples..

Overall, the increment in transnational mobilization forced the Ecuadorian state to consider indigenous peoples in the petroleum policy-making process. This is observed in the formation of the General Direction of the Environment (DIGEMA) in 1984 under the Ministry of Energy and Mines, which encompasses indigenous issues as well as the environment. Furthermore, the lawsuit of the Cofánes against Texaco influenced state policy through its national oil company, Petroecuador. Whereas prior to transnational mobilization oil companies did not, by law, have to consult with indigenous populations in their area of development, since 1993, oil companies, by law, who have blocks within indigenous territories, have to receive written permission from indigenous populations before entering their territory. In addition, prior to the land grant to OPIP in 1992, government administrations did not legally concede land to indigenous communities in the Amazon. Thus, transnational collective action through transnational advocacy networks resulted in procedural change on a state level.

On a transnational level, these cases demonstrate procedural change in INGOS, international funding agencies, and MNCs. Environmental INGOs, which previously organized and made policymaking decisions based on non-indigenous issues have incorporated indigenous committees on their planning boards. This includes organizations such as IBIS Denmark and RAN. Furthermore, these organizations, as observed in the field, make frequent visits and have offices in the indigenous areas to include their concerns in the larger organization goals.[6]

More specifically, the Coalition has been successful in changing World Bank projects and procedures for allocating resources to the Amazon through a $15 million program called the World Bank Environmental Management and Technical Assistance project. The Coalition has also sponsored conferences for international banks, such as Red Bancos (a Washingtong,D.C-based. multi-lateral development bank) and Bank Information Center (BIC), to visit the Amazon and hear testimony from indigenous leaders in order to understand their concerns and influence procedures in funding processes. These contacts with international funding agencies have altered the political opportunity structure for the Amazonian transnational social movement in that they open up avenues policymaking influence and increase resources.

Finally, as suggested by these cases, oil companies such as ARCO Occidental, and Texaco have altered procedures to include indigenous concerns in their policymaking processes. One such example is ARCO. As detailed in Chapter Five, ARCO has created a Technical/Environmental Committee, which meets once a month and includes one member from Petroecuador, one from ARCO, and two members from each of the three local indigenous confederations. Occidental Oil Company has also included indigenous input in their policymaking process through its Community Relations plan. Thus, private, non-state actors have also changed procedural processes due to transnational collective action.

Not only procedures, but also policy outcomes have been changed due to transnational collective action. While transnational collective action is a combined effort between transnational social movement organizations and transnational advocacy networks, these cases suggest that policy change on domestic and MNC levels was more successfully achieved by transnational advocacy networks. This is due, in part, to the ability of the transnational networks to combine domestic mobilizing structures with transnational ones, thus having more access on the domestic level and greater ability to negotiate directly with MNCs in their regions.

Compared to transnational advocacy networks, transnational social movements, due to their ability to mobilize in the international sphere, have had greater success in influencing policy change in international organizations. This is observed not only through these cases, but also in cases of human rights and the environment.[7] These cases illustrate the ability of COICA to communicate with OAS or UN officials to change policy. For example, a major policy outcome for COICA and all indigenous movements was the naming of 1993 as the Year of Indigenous Peoples.

The Ecuadorian transnational advocacy networks had the highest level of success in changing policy and obtaining new policy outcomes from MNCs. Since the state, in these cases, played a minor role, MNCs policies were affected to a greater extent. For instance, Texaco has agreed to a billion-dollar cleanup in the Northern Amazon. ARCO has created educational facilities, health facilities, and technical education programs in Pastaza. Occidental has also provided health facilities, education facilities, and cultural and language preservation programs. These policy outcomes were directly related to the transnational collective action of the indigenous confederations in these regions.

Although the state was involved to a lesser extent than MNCs in this process, there were significant state policy outcomes. In the case of OPIP, the state granted the Quichuas a community-governed territory. In the case of the Cofánes, the state, after some indecision, supported a policy change to implement environmental clean up programs in the Cofán territories. Thus, state-level policy outcomes, while less frequent, are observed.

Finally, behavioral change is the highest level of effectiveness for transnational collective action, according to Sikkink and Keck. This signifies not only episodic or specific case change in outcomes, but also a comprehensive change in discourse, action, and policy outcomes. The greatest area of behavioral change in this study was noted on the level of MNCs. As detailed in Chapter Four, in all cases, MNCs had changed their behavior from the beginning of the 1980s to the present. The transnational collective action process created spaces of negotiation and discourse, which influenced companies to realize that businesses are not only economically, but social and morally responsible (Mendez, Parnell, and Wasserstrom

1998: 13). This process changed MNC overall behavior in the Ecuadorian Amazon from non-inclusive, non-discursive, to inclusive and interested in indigenous population demands and their environment. Thus, an overall trend of behavior change is noted among private, non-state actors.

THE EFFECTS OF TRANSNATIONAL CONTENTIOUS COLLECTIVE ACTION

While some scholars have argued that transnational social movements are displacing the domestic social movement, this project has concluded that domestic social movements are key actors in the transnational collective action process. Domestic social movements, whether on local or regional or national levels, maintain mobilization through transnational advocacy networks based on the strength of their domestic mobilization and ability to attract participants. Furthermore, policy implementation, outcomes, and monitoring are often activities of domestic social movements with the aid of their partners in the advocacy network. Thus, without a well-organized domestic base, neither a transnational advocacy network nor a transnational social movement organization can function successfully.

However, mobilization directly from the local or regional level to the transnational level, as in the case of the Ecuadorian Amazon, does have consequences for the national level. As mobilization increases toward the transnational level, it suffers on the national level. Groups tend to focus their activities and discourse outside of the national realm. This has various consequences that include, 1) a lack of national social movement organization; 2) a separation between leaders on the transnational level, local leaders, and participants; and 3) a competition among local and regional groups for transnational support and resources.

Ecuadorian Amazonian organizations do participate in the national indigenous organization, CONAIE, but have a growing history of division between themselves and their Sierra neighbors. This has caused division within CONAIE and its leadership. Thus, national networks and identity often become weakened in a situation in which one region, in this case the Amazon, has transnationalized, while the other, the Sierra, has not.

Furthermore, within the Amazon, organizations begin to compete for international funds and resources. This was detailed in the Quichua and Siona and Secoya cases, in which the organizations share a territory, but are competing among themselves for resources from Occidental and INGOs. This type of competition not only decentralizes the national organization, but also the regional, Amazonian organization, CONFENIAE.

On the other hand, the transnational social movement organizations are strengthened by the move toward transnational mobilization. As opposed to organizing on regional or national levels, groups in the Amazon have united on a transnational level. This organization has been successful in changing policy on rainforest area issues. However, overall policy change within states may be difficult to achieve when indigenous populations are divided between highland and lowland, as is the case in Ecuador, Peru, Colombia, and Venezuela. Thus, movements that are "born" transnational do not simultaneously signify movements that will be more effective on a national level.

Finally, the increase in transnational collective action in the Amazon may signify new roles for private, non-state actors in the international system. As transnational social movement organizations increase their ability to persuade policies, and as MNCs and INGOs and IGOs become more involved in the bargaining process, the state will experience difficulty in controlling certain policy areas. As mentioned in Chapter Two, we have already begun to see a struggle for power between the state and other non-state, private actors in the area of the environment. Thus, this project implies a revision of the role of the state as the sole authoritative international actor in the international system.

GLOBALIZATION AND AN INTERNATIONAL SOCIETY: SOME CONCLUSIONS

The cases analyzed in this research project suggest that political action above and below the level of the state is occurring with increasing frequency in the international system. However, this does not discount the role of the state as an authoritative international actor. Yet, the strategies and tactics of collective action have changed and developed since the times of Charles Tilly's "British Brawls" in the Eighteenth Century (Tilly 1978). These strategies are highly professionalized and de-centralized among domestic and transnational actors with the targets and policy outcomes not always centrally focused upon the state.

What Sidney Tarrow has called "the strong thesis of globalization" contends that this change in collective action is due to the globalization of culture, the market, and social forces which inevitably knits world processes together.[8] However, weaker theses of globalization contend that the role of the state is adapting to new technological and market advances, which create new spaces of authority for private, non-state actors.[9] This project takes the weaker line, demonstrating that non-state actors do have authoritative policymaking roles and collective action roles in the international system. However, the transnational contentious collective action examined in this study verifies the significance of the domestic organization of social movements and the changing, but still authoritative role of state institutions.

Part of the change in the international system has been attributed to an "international society," or "world civic politics," in which actors from society and from the international system are acting collectively through common networks based upon common beliefs which transpire state borders. Paul Wapner argues that environmental activism is taking place on an international level due to common "civic" beliefs that the environment is important and worth protecting (Wapner 1996). R.B.J. Walker argues that true "world" politics cannot be analyzed via the lens of structures, which break down the process. Rather, he suggests that world politics are far more dynamic than state-based or society-based processes and that these processes frequently cross one another and enter the international realm (Walker 1994). Scholars such as James Riker, Margaret Keck and Kathryn Sikkink, and Thomas Risse-Kappen suggest that the international system is connected to domestic politics through nodes of communication activated by transnational advocacy networks. Each of these arguments contains a common element among them: common international discourse and ideas shared among communities without boundaries.

The transnational Amazonian social movement and its transnational advocacy networks elucidate the complexity of an international society that has united under a common theme to aid the environment and peoples of the Amazon. While many of its activists do not live near the Amazon, nor have they even visited the Amazon, they are transmitted information through the Internet and e-mail and receive information from experts who have worked with indigenous groups in these regions. Although they are not close in spatial measurement, a common discourse and common ideas have been shared and internalized among communities of the world about the concerns of the Amazon and its importance. This does not signify that states are diminishing in power or that a global government is forming, but does imply that a global civil society of concerned, private activists is growing and incorporating themselves into policymaking positions in domestic and transnational levels.

Therefore, this project suggests a re-interpretation of the international system, incorporating elements of domestic politics and international politics, rather than a separation of structures. Furthermore, these case studies demonstrate the need to include international economic actors and market forces in studies of social movements and transnational collective action. While previous studies highlight the roles of INGOs in the transnational collective action process, these case studies illustrate the significance of MNCs and their influence on policy outcomes both domestically and internationally. As the international system continues to develop, these case studies and this model will be and are applicable to not only the South American Amazonian region, but to all regions in which social actors have mobilized beyond state borders to achieve change inside and outside of their communities.

NOTES

[1] See Tarrow, Sidney (1994). *Power in Movement.* Cambridge: Cambridge University Press; McAdam, Doug, John D. McCarthy, and Mayer N. Zald, "Opportunities, Mobilizing Structures, and Framing Processes - Toward a Synthetic, Comparative Perspective on Social Movements" In McAdam, Doug, John D. McCarthy, and Mayer N. Zald (1996). *Comparative Perspectives on Social Movements.* Cambridge: Cambridge University Press; Tilly, Charles (1978). *From Mobilization to Revolution.* New York: McGraw-Hill, Inc.

[2] See Tarrow, Sidney (1994). *Power in Movement.* Cambridge: Cambridge University Press: pp.54–57.

[3] The term authority refers to the traditional realist approach to International Relations in which states are the only forces of influence and change in the international system. This approach does not assume a state-centric international system, but rather one in which states and other non-state actors hold power and have the ability to change, alter, and influence international and domestic systems.

[4] See Restrepo G., Marco (1993). "El Problema de la Frontera en la Construcción del Espacio Amazónico." In Lucy Ruiz. *Amazonia: Escenarios y Conflictos.* Quito: CEDIME.

[5] For more information on these issues, see Chapter Three.

[6] This was witnessed in Quito, Ecuador during field research. RAN representatives often flew to Quito and traveled to their project areas. After these site visits, they discussed with local leaders how they could include their demands in the larger organizational framework. IBIS Denmark, which primarily works with OPIP, has an office in Quito and in Puyo, Pastaza.

[7] See Wapner, Paul (1996). *Environmental Activism and World Civic Politics.* New York: SUNY Press; and Jackie Smith, et al. (1998).

[8] See Mittelman, James H.(1996). *Globalization: Critical Reflections.* Boulder: Lynne Rienner Publishers.

[9] See Keck and Sikkink (1998).

Interview List

FORMAL INTERVIEWS

Jorge Alvarado, President, Federation of Indigenous Peoples of Napo (FOIN)—April 24, 1997

Ampam, Director, World Bank Project on the Confederation of Indigenous and African Ecuadorian Peoples—October 30, 1996

Segundo Anrrango, Representative, Confederation of Indigenous Peoples of Imbabura (FICI)—October 30, 1996

Juan Aulestía, consultant, CONAIE—November 8, 1996

Rodolfo Aznar, Director of Communications, COICA—February 19, 1997

Lucía Burgos, Amazon Specialist, Fundacion Natura—February 21, 1997 and trip to Napo on April 24, 1997

Dr. Alfredo Lozano Castro, National Congress Representative—November 4, 1996

Johnson Cerda, Quichua from Federation of Indigenous Peoples of Sucumbios (FOISE) and representative in the National Secretariat for Indigenous Affairs—November 4, 1996 and January 20, 1997

Marco Correa, Engineer, Ministry of Energy and Mines—April 24, 1997

Marcelino Chumpi, Shuar representative, National Secretariat for Indigenous Affairs—November 25, 1996

Luís Enrique Cuuambi, Vice-President, Confederation of Indigenous Peoples of the Ecuadorian Amazon (CONFENIAE)—November 8, 1996

Terry R. Davidson, Cultural Attache, Embassy of the United States in Ecuador—January 15, 1998

Manuel Echeverría, Engineer and Director of Community Relations, Occidental Oil Company—November 20, 1996
Paul Fritz, Ecuador Representative, USAID—April 11, 1997

Paulina Garzon, President, Accion Ecologica, March 17, 1997

Hans Hoffmeyer, Coordinator, IBIS-Denmark in Ecuador—March 10, 1997

Victor Hugo, COMUNIDEC—March 26, 1997

María Elena Jervis, Amazon Project Representative, Fundacion Antisana—February 19, 1997

Kar, Shuar Representative, May 13, 1998

Ariruma Kowii, Professor of Quichua and consultant to the CONAIE—October 30, 1996, November 13, 1996

Alfredo Lozano, consultant to National Congress Representative Luis Macas from Loja (Partido Pachakutik)—November 4, 1996

Sixto Méndez, Manager of Health, Environment, and Safety, ARCO Oil Company—January 19, 1997

Mariano Morocho, Secretary, National Secretariat for Indigenous Affairs—November 4, 1996

Marcelo Naranjo, Professor of Sociology and Anthropology, Catholic University of Ecuador—November 7, 1996

David Parra, President, Fundacion Antisana—February 19, 1997

Galo Ramon, Director, COMUNIDEC—a non-profit Ecuadorian NGO—November 13, 1996

General Rodriguez Lara, Military Leader of Ecuador (1972-1976), May 12, 1998

Rodrigo Santiago de la Cruz, Confederation of Indigenous Peoples of the Amazon Basin (COICA)—November 19, 1996 and February 19, 1997

Cristóbal Tapuy, former-President, CONAIE—November 26, 1996

Yolanda Terán, consultant, National Confederation of Indigenous Peoples of Ecuador (CONAIE)—October 30, 1996

Elvira Vallejo, former-Director, Fundacion Natura—January 5, 1997

Vicentes, Representative, Confederation of Indigenous Peoples of the Ecuadorian Sierra (ECUARUNARI)—November 13, 1996

Leonardo Viteri, Director, Amazanga Institute of Science and Technology—March 7, 1997

Shannon Wright, Representative for the Amazonian region, Rainforest Action Network (RAN)—November 16, 1996

Carmen Yamberla, President, Federation of Indigenous Peoples of Imbabura (FICI)—July 18, 1996

INFORMAL INTERVIEWS/CONVERSATIONS

Adrián Bonilla, Professor of Social Sciences, Facultad Latinoamericano de Ciencias Sociales (FLACSO) Ecuador

Dr. Jaime Borja, former-President of Ecuador

Raúl Carrera, Professor of International Relations, La Universidad de San Francisco de Quito

Dr. Oswaldo Hurtado, former-President of Ecuador

Dr. Jamil Mahuad, President of Ecuador

Ignacio Pérez Arteta, former-Minister of Agriculture under President Sixto Duran Ballen

José Sánchez Parga, Professor of Political Science, La Universidad Catolica, Quito, Ecuador

Melina Selverston, Director, The Coalition for Amazonian Peoples and their Environment

Gustavo Vallejo, consultant, Ministry of Tourism

Raúl Vallejo, former-Minister of Education under President Borja and Professor of Arts and Letters in La Universidad Andina, Quito, Ecuador

Deborah Yashar, Professor of Politics, Princeton University

OBSERVATIONS

Acción Ecológica

ARCO Oil Company

Fundación Antisana

Fundación Natura

Occidental Oil Company

The National Confederation of Indigenous Peoples of Ecuador (CONAIE)
The Coalition for Amazonian Peoples and their Environment

The Confederation of Indigenous Peoples of the Ecuadorian Amazon (CONFENIAE)

The Confederation of Indigenous Peoples of the Ecuadorian Sierra (ECUARUNARI)

The Coordinator for Indigenous Peoples of the Amazon Basin (COICA)

The Federation of Indigenous Peoples of Napo (FOIN)

The Federation of Indigenous Peoples of Sucumbios (FOISE)

The Organization of Indigenous Peoples of Pastaza (OPIP)

Explanation of the Methodology and Interview Process

THIS PROJECT RELIED ON PRIMARY RESOURCES, SUCH AS ARCHIVAL OR newspaper information, secondary resources, such as academic journal articles, formal and informal interviews, and observation of the institutions and people involved in the transnational process. With regard to primary and secondary resources, these resources were obtained in the United States and Ecuador. The primary resources of indigenous confederations were obtained through direct, oral permission from indigenous confederation leaders. In the case of Amazonian indigenous confederations, I was permitted direct access to the archives of The Confederation of Indigenous Nationalities of the Ecuadorian Amazon, The Federation of Indigenous Peoples of Napo (FOIN), The Indigenous Organizations of Sucumbíos, Ecuador (FOISE), and The Coordinator of Indigenous Organizations in the Amazon Basin (COICA), and the Coalition of Amazonian Peoples and their Environment. Archival resources from other confederations such as the Organization of Secoya Indians (OISE), the Organization of Siona Indians (ONISE), and the Organization of Indigenous Peoples of Pastaza (OPIP) through the archival systems of non-governmental organizations, namely Fundación Natura, Acción Ecológica, and Rainforest Action Network (RAN). In these cases, the NGOs kept files on their records and communications with the indigenous confederations. Due to the underdevelopment of technology and the lack of administrative organization of many Amazonian indigenous confederations, archives in some cases do not exist, or are extremely unorganized. However, every attempt was made to compile accurate and substantial archival information.

The primary resources from Amazonian and international NGOs were collected directly from these NGO offices with their permission. Also, MNC primary evidence was obtained from Ecuadorian and U.S.-based headquarters. Both parties were very helpful and open with regard to their archival evidence. Few government documents exist on transnational networks or the indigenous question in Ecuador. However, some documents were obtained through interview contact with government officials. In general, Ecuador's national archival system is incomplete and unorganized.

The empirical evidence for this project, given its analysis of networks that often times are of an oral or spatially distant (not face-to-face) nature, was obtained via interviews. These interviews were conducted in Spanish in formal and informal atmospheres. The interviewees were given the option of anonymity. Those who chose this option are not listed in the Appendix. However their information was a substantial contribution to the project. Moreover, the interviewees were asked if taping the interviews was possible. Some allowed cassette tapes, others allowed note taking and others did not allow any materials in the interview session. The formal interview was conducted in the office of an indigenous leader, NGO or INGO leader, MNC employee, government official, or academic specialist. These interviews lasted between one hour and five hours, and were directed by a list of pre-compiled questions, which focused on the indicators listed in the hypotheses of Chapter Two. The questions were open-ended in nature and all interviews ended with suggestions for other individuals in the process with whom I could speak.

The informal interview was utilized throughout the fieldwork process to gain perspective on the information that I was obtaining. For example, although President Borja did not provide me with specific information on case studies, he did inform me of the general "feeling" of his administration towards policies, or shed light on this decision-making processes. While this information did no prove useful in factual documentation, it did enhance my perspective as an objective researcher.

Finally, in the preceding Appendix attachment, I list institutions, which allowed me to observe their offices and daily functioning. This observation process was extremely helpful in order to determine the strength of informal networks among transnational movement or advocacy network participants. In this sense, I gained an understanding of the amount of phone calls made to members or participants, and the familiarity of participants with one another. Given the nature of the study—one of social networks among peoples of sometimes-great distances—observations of NGO, MNC, and indigenous confederation offices were very significant to my understanding of the transnational process and the connections among participants.

As mentioned in Chapter Two, the dangers of bias are always existent in any research project. Moreover, the Amazon is one of the more under-developed sectors of the world, where documented information is difficult to find. For this reason, I employed an array of methodologies in order to capture the most actual and correct evidence as possible.

Interview Questions

SAMPLE QUESTIONNAIRE TO NGO OR INDIGENOUS CONFEDERATION REPRESENTATIVES

1. Name and title of the person

2. History of the person in the organization. How many years have they been involved in the organization? Have they been involved in other organizations and if so, which? What different positions and responsibilitites have they held in the position?

3. When did their organization establish international contacts with other actors?

4. Does the organization have direct contact with international actors such as INGOs, MNCs, multi-lateral development banks, or other such international actors?

5. Describe the contacts that you have with NGOs, either national or international. Do these contacts include funding, other types of resources, communications technology? Are these contacts direct with the other organization or indirect?

6. With which NGOs do you have contact? Where are they from?

7. Does your organization have any contact with oil companies? If

so, which ones? Since what time-period? What is the current situation with this oil company?

8. Have there been any direct communications with the oil company(ies)? If so, have there been any negotitations? If not, why have there been no direct communications with the oil company(ies)?

9. Do you think that your organization has changed since these international contacts—either with NGOs or with oil companies? How so?

10. Do you coordinate policies and strategies with international governmental or non-governmental organizations? How so?

11. Do you think that these organizations have any influence over the Ecuadorian government?

12. How does the Ecuadorian government affect your organization?

13. How much do you or people from your organization travel abroad?

14. Are international contacts important for your organization?

15. What are the political goals of your organization? How do you obtain these goals—through what kinds of forms of mobilization strategies?

16. What, if any, forms of communication does your organization employ?

17. How often do leaders of the organization communicate to its members/community? Is there a certain form of communication used over others?

18. Is there anyone else with whom you recommend I speak?

SAMPLE QUESTIONARRE TO OIL COMPANY REPRESENTATIVES

1. Name and title.

2. The history of the person in the company. How many years have they worked there? What different positions did he/she hold?

3. The history of the company in the Amazon and which block it occupied. The amount of resources invested in this endeavor.

4. What are the company's futures plans in the Amazon?

5. Does the company maintain contacts with indigenous confederations? If so, describe them. If not, why?

6. Do they have contacts with NGO representatives and if so, how? With which NGOs do they communicate?

7. Has the company had any negotiations with indigenous confederations? Which? When? How did they function? What were the results?

8. What influences the operations of the company in the Amazon—indigenous organizations, the national government, NGOs?

9. What has been the role of the government in oil development in the Amazon?

10. What has been the role of the government with regard to indigenous issue-areas?

11. What influences the company to enter negotiations with an indigenous organization?

12. Have you noted a change in your company since contacts with indigenous organizations have been established? If so, how?

13. With whom else should I speak on this subject?

References

Acción Ecológica (September 1996). *Alerta Verde.* "Occidental Petroleum Company."

Atawari, Kar (May 13, 1998). *Interview.*

Ayala Mora, Enrique (1993). *Resumen de Historia del Ecuador.* Quito: Corporación Editora Nacional.

Barker, Greg. (Arpil 19, 1993). "Ecuador: Troubled Oil Sector." *Business Latin America*:5–6.

Brogan, Christopher. (1984). "The Retreat from Oil Nationalism in Ecuador. 1976–1983."in *University of London Institute of Latin American Studies Working Papers.* London: University of London.

Brysk, Alison (October 1993). "From Above and Below: Social Movements, the International System, and Human Rights in Argentina." *Comparative Political Studies.* 26(3):259–285.

——— (1994). "Acting Globally: Indian Rights and International Politics in Latin America." in D.L. Van Cott. *Indigenous Peoples and Democracy in Latin America.* New York: St. Martin's Press.

——— (1994). "Latin American Indian Rights Movements at the United Nations." Paper presented at the University of Notre Dame *conference on "Transnational Social Movements and International Organizations,"* April 22–24, 1994.

Burger, Julian (1987). *Report from the Frontier: The State of the World's Indigenous Peoples.* London: Zed Books, Ltd.

Calderon, Fernando, Alejandro Piscitelli, and Jose Luis Reyna (1992). "Social Movements: Actors, Theories, Expectations." In A. Escobar and Sonia E. Alvarez. *The Making of Social Movements in Latin America*. Boulder, Colorado: Westview Press.

Capitol Hill Hearing Testimony. Testimony April 20, 1994 from Congressperson Robert C. Torricelli, Chairman Subcommittee on Western Hemisphere Affairs Hous Foreign Affairs Committee.

Cerny, Philip G. (1995). "Globalization and the Changing Logic of Collective Action" *International Organization* 49(4): 595–625.

Chong, Dennis (1991). *Collective Action and the Civil Rights Movement*. Chicago: University of Chicago Press.

Coalition for Amazonian Peoples and their Environment (1996). *Declaration of Mission*. Washington, D.C.

Coalition for Amazonian Peoples and their Environment (1995). "Amazon Update #9: December 15, 1995."

Coalition for Amazonian Peoples and their Environment (1996). "Amazon Aupdate #20: December 15, 1996."

Coalition For Amazonian Peoples and their Environment (1996). "Amazon Update #16: August 15, 1996."

"COICA: En la Búsqueda del Desarrollo Autónomo y Sustentable." *Punto de Vista:563*.

COICA (1993). "Es Necesario Detener el Genocidio!" *Comunicado de Prensa, COICA Archive*.

COICA (July 21, 1993). "La Amazonia es También Pueblos Indígenas." *COICA Archive*.

COICA (July 1993). "Indígenas Amazónicos Demandan Investigación de la CIDH en Brasil y Peru." *COICA Archive*.

COICA (September 5, 1994). "COICA Pide Comisión Internacional Investigue Caso Ashaninkas." *COICA Archive*.

COICA (September 26, 1994). "Indígenas Defienden La Propiedad de Sus Conociemientos." *COICA Archive*.

COICA (November 11, 1994). "Piden Investigar Matanzas Indígenas Brasil y Peru." *COICA Archive*.

COICA (November 12, 1994). "Jefes Indígenas Alistan Documento Que Presentarán en Cumbre de las Américas." *COICA Archive*.

COICA (November 30, 1994). "Carta Abierta a los Presidentes Americanos." *COICA Archive*.

COICA (December 5, 1994). "Pueblos Indio Entrgaran Reclamos a Cumbre Presidencial." *COICA Archive*.

COICA (February 22, 1995). "Letter from Indian Law Resource Center." *COICA Archive*.

COICA (July 10, 1995). "Indígenas de Zona Fronteriza Se Reunieran en Bolivia." *COICA Archive*.

COICA (July 12, 1995). "Ecuador-Peru: Indígenas de Ecuador y Peru se Reunen Por la Paz." *COICA Archive.*

COICA (July 19, 1995). "Indígenas del Peru y Ecuador Piden la Paz." *COICA Archive.*

COICA (June 24, 1996). "Indígenas Rechazan Patente de Bregaje Sagrado y Ritual Amazónico." *COICA Archive.*

de la Cruz, Rodrigo, Asistente Técnico, COICA. *Interview.* February 19, 1997.

Colitt, Raymond. (August 2, 1993). "Fueling Petroleum Output." *Business Latin America* 28:6.

—— (Nov. 29, 1993). "Business Outlook: Ecuador." *Business Latin America* 28: 4–5.

Conaghan, Catherine M. and Rosario Espinal. (1990). "Unlikely Transitions to Uncertain Regimes? Democracy without Compromise in the Dominican Republic and Ecuador." *Journal of Latin American Studies*, 1990. 22: 553–574.

Conaghan, Catherine (1995). "Politicians against Parties: Discord and Disconnection in Ecuador's Party System." In S. Mainwaring and T.R. Scully,eds. *Building Democratic Insitutions: Party Systems in Latin America.* Stanford: Stanford University Press.

—— (1994). "Democracy that Matters: The Search for Authenticity, Legitimacy, and Civic Competence in the Andes." *Project Latin America 2000 Series.* Working Ppaer #1: University of Notre Dame.

—— and John M. Malloy (1994). *Unsettling Statecraft: Democracy and Neoliberalism in the Central Andes.* Pittsburgh: University of Pittsburgh Press.

CONAIE (1989). *Las Nacionalidades Indígenas en el Ecuador: Nuestro Proceso Organizativo.* Quito: Editorial Tincui-CONAIE, and Editorial Abya-Yala.

Conca, Ken (1994). "Rethinking the Ecology-Sovereignty Debate." *Millennium*: Journal of International Studies 23(3):701–711.

Conger Lind, Amy (1992). "Power, Gender, and Development: Popular Women's Organizations and the Politics of Needs in Ecuador." in A. Escobar and S.E. Alvarez. *The Making of Social Movements in Latin America.* Boulder: Westview Press.

"Cuarto Congreso de la CONAIE Mantiene Independencia de Partidos Politicos." 1993 *Congress Notes from CONAIE.*

Cutler, Claire A. (1995). "Global Capitalism and Liberal Myths: Dispute Settlement in Private International Trade Relations" *Millennium: Journal of International Studies* 24(3):377–397.

Cutler, Claire, Virginia Haufler, and Tony Porter (1996). "Private Authority and International Regimes" Paper Presented at the *Workshop on Private Power, Public Power, and International Regimes*, San Diego, CA, April 16, 1996.

Díaz-Polanco, Héctor (Summer 1992). "Indian Communities and the Quincentenary." *Latin American Perspectives*. 19(3):18–21.

Donnelly, Jack (1994). "Human Rights and International Organizations: States, Sovereignty, and the International Community." In F. Kratochwil and E.D. Mansfield. *International Organization: A Reader*. New York: Harper Collins College Publishers.

"Ecuador: Amerindians Give Conditions for Continued Oil Drilling." *Inter Press Service*. December 14, 1993.

"Ecuador Indians Seek End to Amazon Oil Drilling." *Rueters*. October 18, 1993.

"Ecuador Indians Sue Texaco for Rainforest Contamination." *United Press International*. November 2, 1993.

"Ecuador: Indigenous People Reject New Agrarian Law." *Inter Press Service*. June 3, 1994.

"Ecuador: Skin Diseases Plague Forest Inhabitants." *Inter Press Service*. March 30, 1994.

Eckstein, Susan,ed. (1989). *Power and Popular Protest*. Berkeley: University of California Press.

El Comercio (May 13, 1997). "Texaco: La Limpieza en Entredicho:" C12.

The Energy Economist. (July 1995)."Ecuador":12–14.

Escobar, Arturo and Sonia E. Alvarez (1992). *The Making of Social Movements in Latin America*. Boulder, Colorado: Westview Press.

Evans, Peter (1995). *Embedded Autonomy: States and Industrial Transformation*. Princeton: Princeton University Press.

Fernández, Edwin (January 24, 1994). "Indígenas Piden Moratoria" *El Comercio*: D8.

Field, Les (1991). "Ecuador's Pan-Indian Uprising, NACLA Report on the Americas. 25(3):38–44.

Fundación Natura (1996). *La Actividad Petrolera en el Ecuador*. Quito: Ediciones Abya-Yala.

Gaete, Sergio. "Ecuador: Ecologists Announce International Boycott Against Texaco." *Inter Press Service*. May 3, 1993.

Gamson, William A. (1992). "The Social Psychology of Collective Action." in A. Morris and C. McClury Mueller,eds.,*Frontiers in Social Movement Theory*. New Haven: Yale University Press.

Goldstone, Jack (1991). "An Analytical Framework," In J.A. Goldstone, T.R. Gurr, and F. Moshirir. *Revolutions of the Latin Twentieth Century*. Boulder: Westview Press.

"Government Claims 3% Growth This Year." *Latin America Regional Reports: Andean Group*. August 4, 1994.

Gurr, Ted Robert (1970). *Why Men Rebel*. Princeton: Princeton University Press.

—— (1993). *Minorities At Risk: A Global View of Ethnopolitical Conflicts*. Washington, D.C.: United States Institute of Peace.

—— and Barbara Harff (1994). *Ethnic Conflict in World Politics*. Boulder: Westview Press.

Haas, Ernst B. (1983). "Words Can Hurt You; Or, Who Said What to Whom About Regimes." In S.D. Krasner,ed. *International Regimes*. Ithaca: Cornell University Press.

Hardin, Russell (1982). *Collective Action*. Baltimore: Johns Hopkins University Press.

Haufler, Virginia (1993). "Crossing the Boundary Between Public and Private: International Regimes and Non-State Actors." in V. Rittberger, ed. *Regime Theory and International Relations*. Oxford: Clarendon/Oxford University Press.

—— (1996). "Private International Regimes and Corporate Norms." Paper Presented at the *Workshop on "Private Power, Public Power, and International Regimes,"* April 16, 1996, San Diego, California.

Hey, Jeanne A. "Foreign Policy Options Under Dependence: A Theoretical Evaluation with Evidence from Ecuador." *Journal of Latin American Studies*, 1993. 25: 543–574.

Holmstrom, David. "Ecuador Indians Fight for Forests." *The Christian Science Monitor*. June 16, 1993: 9.

Ibarra, Alicia (1992). *Los Indígenas y El Estado en el Ecuador*. Quito: CEDIME.

Imig, Doug and Sidney Tarrow (1996). "The Europeanization of Movements? Contentious Politics and the European Union, October 1983–March 1995." Paper Presented at the *ECSA Annual Conference* at Charleston, S.C..

"Indians Denounce 'Deal' With Texaco." *Latin American Weekly Report*. January 27, 1994: 28.

Jenkins, J. Craig, and Kurt Schock (1992). "Global Structures and Political Processes in the Study of Domestic Political Conflict: *Annual Review of Sociology*: 18:161–185.

Jochnick, Chris (1995). "Amazon Oil Offensive." *Multinational Monitor* 26(1–2):2–10.

Kane, Joe (1995). *Savages.* New York: Alfred A. Knopf.

—— (May 2, 1994). "Moi Goes to Washington." *The New Yorker*: 74–81.

—— (September 27, 1993). "Letter from the Amazon." *The New Yorker*: 54–79.

Keck, Margaret and Kathryn Sikkink (1998). *Activists Beyond Borders.* Ithaca: Cornell University Press.

—— (1998). "Transnational Advocacy Networks in the Movement Society." in David S. Meyer and Sidney Tarrow, eds. *The Social Movement Society.* Oxford: Rowman and Littlefield.

Kimerling, Judith. (1991). *Amazon Crude.* National Resources Defense Council.

Klandermans, Bert (1992). "The Social Construction of Protest and Multiorganizational Fields," in A. Morris and C. McClury Mueller, eds., *Frontiers in Social Movement Theory.* New Haven: Yale University Press.

Krasner, Stephen D. (1983). "Structural Causes and Regime Consequences: Regimes as Intervening Variables." In S.D. Krasner, ed. *International Regimes.* Ithaca: Cornell University Press.

Kremling Gómez, Desider (1997). "El Desarrollo Sustentable Amazónico: Una Discusión a partir de las Políticas del Tratado de Cooperación Amazónica." in Doris Herrera, ed. *La Cuenca Amazónica de Cara Al Nuevo Siglo.* Quito: FLACSO.

Lichback, Mark Irving (1994). *The Rebel's Dilemma.* Ann Arbor: University of Michigan Press.

Lipschutz, Ronnie D. (1992). "Reconstructing World Politics: The Emergence of Global Civil Society." *Millennium* 21(3):389–420.

——, John D. McCarthy, and Mayer N. Zald (1996). *Comparative Perspectives on Social Movements.* Cambridge: Cambridge University Press.

"Los Ecuatorianos Eligen Nuevo President." *El Diario/LaPrensa.* May 17, 1992: 9.

Macas, Luis (1991). El Levantamiento Indígena Visto Por Sus Protagonistas. Ecuador: *Instituto Científico de Culturas Indígenas.*

Maiguashca, Bice (1996). "The Role of Ideas in A Changing World Order: The International Indigenous Movement, 1975–1990." *CERLAC Occasional Papers, Number 4.* Ontario: York University Center for Research on Latin America and the Caribbean.

Martz, John D. (January 1988). "Instability in Ecuador." *Current History*:17–20.

——. "Instability in Ecuador." *Current History* January 1988: 17–20.

—— (1987). *Politics and Petroleum in Ecuador*. New Brunswick, N.J.: Transaction Books.

Marx Ferree, Myra (1992). "The Political Context of Rationalitiy: Rational Choice Theory and Resource Mobilization," in A. Morris and C. McClury Mueller, eds., *Frontiers in Social Movement Theory*. New Haven: Yale University Press.

McAdam, Doug and Dieter Rucht (1993). "The Cross National Diffusion of Movement Ideas," *Annals of the American Academy of Political and Social Science* 528:56–74.

McAdam, Doug (1996). "Conceptual Origins, Current Problems, Future Directions." in Doug McAdam, John D. McCarthy, and Mayer N.Zald (eds.). *Comparative Perspectives on Social Movements*. Cambridge: Cambridge University Press.

——, John D. McCarthy, and Mayer N. Zald (1996). *Comparative Perspectives on Social Movements*. Cambridge: Cambridge University Press.

McClurg Mueller, Carol (1992). "Building Social Movement Theory," in A. Morris and C. McClury Mueller,eds. *Frontiers in Social Movement Theory*. New Haven: Yale University Press.

Melucci, Alberto (1980). "The New Social Movements: A Theoretical Approach," *Social Science Information* 19:199–226.

Mendez, Sixto, Jennifer Parnell, and Robert Wasserstrom (June 1998). "Seeking Common Ground." *Environment:*40 (5):pp.13–45.

Menéndez-Carrión, Amparo (1989). "La Democracia en el Ecuador: Desafios, Dilemas, y Perspectivas." Quito: *FLACSO: Documentos de Trabajo*: No.3.

Meyer, Carrie A. (1993). "Environmental NGOs in Ecuador: An Economic Analysis of Institutional Change." *The Journal of Developing Areas* 27 (January):191–210.

Meyer, David S. and Sidney Tarrow (1998). "A Movement Society: Contentious Politics for a New Century." in David S. Meyer and Sidney Tarrow, eds. *The Social Movement Society*. Oxford: Rowman and Littlefield.

Mittelman, James H.,ed. *Globalization: Critical Reflections*. Boulder: Lynne Rienner.

Olson, Mancur (1965). *The Logic of Collective Action*. Cambridge: Harvard University Press.

Ortiz, Benjamin. "The End of a Long Sleep." *Worldpaper.*: 8.

Pandor, R. Jordan. (1990). "Desarrollo y Poblaciones Indígenas de América Latina y el Caribe." *Instituto Indígenista Americano and the FAO*.

Peterson, M.J. (1992). "Transnational Activity, International Society and World Politics. *Millennium* 21(3):371–388.

Psacharopoulos, George and Harry Anthony Patrinos, eds. (1994). *Indigenous People and Poverty in Latin America.* Washington,D.C.: The World Bank.

Puchala, Donald J. and Raymond F. Hopkins (1983). "International Regimes: Lessons From Inductive Analysis." In S.D. Krasner,ed. *International Regimes.* Ithaca: Cornell University Press.

Putnam, Robert (1994). *Making Democracy Work.* Cambridge: Cambridge University Press.

―――― (1988). "Diplomacy and Domestic Politics: The Logic of Two-Level Games." *International Organization* 42:427–460.

Rainforest Action Network (RAN) (1995). "Protect-an-Acre Grants Given in Amazonian Countries." Report from the World Wide Web RAN citation.

Ramon, Galo (1992). *Actores de Una Decada Ganada: Tribus, Comunidades, y Campesinos en la Modernidad.* Quito: COMU-NIDEC.

Raustiala, Kal (forthcoming). "State and Non-State Actors in International Environmental Regimes." Draft Paper.

Restrepo G., Marco (1993). "El Problema de La Frontera en la Construcción del Espacio Amazónico." in Lucy Ruiz M. *Amazonía:Escenarios y Conflictos.* Quito: Abya-Yala.

Rodriguez Lara, General. *Interview.* May 12, 1998.

Riker, James V. (1996). "Inter-Societal Linkages in a Global Civil Society: Transcending the State for Global Governance?" Paper presented at the *37th Annual Meeting of International Studies Association,* San Diego, California, April 16–20, 1996.

Risse-Kappen, Thomas (1995). *Bringing Transnational Relations Back In: Non-State Actors, Domestic Structures, and International Institutions.* Cambridge: Cambridge University Press.

Rochon, Thomas R. and Daniel A. Mazmanian (1993). "Social Movements and Policy Process," *Annals of the American Academy of Political and Social Science* 528:75–87.

Ruggie, John Gerard, ed. (1993). *Multilateralism Matters.* New York: Columbia University Press.

Salacuse, Maria. (1993)"The Revisionist Analysis of the Indigenous Movement of Resistence in Ecuador: From the Spanish Conquest to the Present." *Latin American Certificate Thesis.* May 5, 1993.

Sanchez Parga, José (1990). *Étnia, Poder y Diferencia.* Quito:Abya-Yala.

——— (1997). *Globalización, Gobernabilidad y Cultura*. Quito: Abya-Yala.

Sawyer, Suzana (Spring 1996). "Indigenous Initiatives and Petroleum Politics in the Ecuadorian Amazon" *Cultural Survival Quarterly*:Spring 1996:26– 30.

Scurrah, Martin J. (1995). "Lessons From Environmental Struggles in the Andes" Paper Presented at the 1995 *Meeting of the Latin American Studies Association*, Washington, D.C., September 28–30, 1995.

Selverston, Melina, ed. (June 26–July 1, 1996). *Annual Meeting Report*. Quito, Ecuador: The Coalition for Amazonian Peoles and their Environment.

———, Director (April 1996), The Coalition for Amazonian Peoples and their Environment, *Interview*.

———, ed. (December 15, 1996). *Amazon Update:9*.

——— (1994). "The Politics of Culture: Indigenous Peoples and the State in Ecuador." in D.L. Van Cott. *Indigenous Popeles and Democracy in Latin America*. New York: St. Martin's Press.

Serrano, Fernando. (1993). *The Transformation of the Indian Peoples of theEcuadorian Amazon into Political Actors and its Effects on the State's Modernization Policies*. Master's Thesis. University of Florida.

Seventh Generation Fund. (January 1994). *The Struggle of the Organizationof Indigenous Peoples of Pastaza - OPIP*. Newsletter.

Silva, Eduardo (1996). "From Dictatorship to Democracy: The Business-State Nexus in Chile's Economic Transformation, 1975–1994." *Comparative Politics* April 1996:299–320.

Smith, Jackie, R. Pagnucco, and W. Romeril (1994). "Transnational Social Movement Organizations in the Global Political Arena." *Volutas* (Summer).

Smith, Richard Chase (1996). "La Pólitica de la Diversidad: COICA y las Federacioens Étnicas de la Amazonía." in S. Varese,ed. *Pueblos Indios, Soberanía, y Globalismo*. Quito: Abya-Yala.

Snow, David E. and Robert D. Benford (1992). "Master Frames and Cycles of Protest," in A. Morris and C. McClury Mueller, eds., *Frontiers in Social Movement Theory*. New Haven: Yale University Press.

Stavenhaggen, Rodolfo (Winter 1992). "Challenging the Nation-State in Latin America." *Journal of International Affairs*. 45(2):421–440.

——— (October 1984) "Los Movimientos Étnicos y El Estado Nacional En América Latina." *Desarrollo: Una Publicación de Colombia Para América Latina*. Año XVIII. (81)19–26.

Stopford, John M., Susan Strange, with John S. Henley (1991). *Rival States, Rival Firms: Competitin for World Market Shares.* Cambridge: Cambridge University Press.

Strange, Susan (1996). *The Retreat of the State: The Diffusion of Power in the World Economy.* Cambridge: Cambridge University Press.

Switkes, Glenn. (Sept/Oct. 1994). "The People vs. Texaco." *NACLA Report on the Americas.* 28(2):6–10.

Tarrow, Sidney (1994). *Power in Movement: Social Movements, Collective Action, and Politics.* Cambridge: Cambridge University Press.

—— (1996). "Fishnets, Internets, and Catnets: Globalization and Transnational Collective Action:" Working Paper 78 (March). Madrid: *Instituto Juan March de Esudios e Investigaciones.*

—— (1998). *Power in Movement: Social Movements and Contentious Politics,*rev. ed. Cambridge: Cambridge University Press.

Tilly, Charles (1978). *From Mobilization to Revolution.* New York: McGraw-Hill Publishing.

Treakle, Kay (1998). "Ecuador: Structural Adjustment and Indigenous and Environmental Resistance." in J.Fox and L. David Brown,eds. *The Struggle for Accountability: The World Bank, NGOs, and Grassroots Movements.* Boston: MIT Press.

Tsebelis, George (1990). *Nested Games.* Berkeley: University of California Press.

Vallejo, Raúl (1996). "Crónica Mestiza del Nuevo Pachakutik." *Latin American Studies Center*, University of Maryland, College Park. Working Paper No.2.

Van Cott, Donna Lee (1993). "Ecuador: Is Modernization Enough?" *Hemisphere.* Summer/Fall 1993: 16.

—— (1993). "Indigenismo Shakes the Andes." *North-South.* October-November 1993: 43–44).

—— (1994)."A Separate Peace." *Hemisfile.* September/October 1994 5 (5): 10.

——. (1994). "Violence, Rebellion in Ecuador." *The Journal of Commerce.* July 14, 1994.

Varea, Anamaría (1995). *Marea Negra en la Amazonía.* Quito: Ediciones Abya- Yala.

Varese, Stefano (1996). *Pueblos Indios, Soberania, y Globalismo.* Quito: Abya-Yala.

Viotti, Paul R. and Mark V. Kauppi (1993). *International Relations Theory: Realism, Pluralism, Globalism.* New York: MacMillian Publishing Company.

Viteri, Leonardo. *Interview.* March 7, 1997.

Walker, R.B.J. (1994). "Social Movements/World Politics."*Millenium: Journal of International Studies*: 23(3):669–700.

Wapner, Paul (April 1995). "Politics Beyond the State: Environmental Activism and World Civic Politics." *World Politcs* 47:311–340.

——— (1996). "Bringing Society Back In: Environmental Governance and World Sociology" Paper Presented at the *Annual Meeting of the International Studies Association*, San Diego, CA, April, 1996.

——— (1996). *Environmental Activism and World Civic Politics*. New York: SUNY Press.

Whitten, Norman E. and Diego Quiroga, with P. Rafael Savoia (1995). Afro-Latin Americans Today: No Longer Invisible. London: *Minority Rights Group*.

Wilmer, Franke (1993). *The Indigenous Voic in World Politics*. Newbury Park: SAGE Publications.

Wright, Shannon (1996). "Occidental Petroleum Hammers the Amazon." *World Rainforest Action Report*: 13(2).

Yashar, Deborah J. (1998). "Contesting Citizenship: Indigenous Movements and Democracy in Latin America." *Comparative Politics* (October):23–42.

Young, Oran R. (1994). "The Politics of Regime Formation: Managing Natural Resources and the Environment" In F. Kratochwil and E.D. Mansfield. *International Organization: A Reader*. New York Harper Collins College Publishers.

Zamosc, Leon (1994). "Agrarian Protest and the Indian Movement in the Ecuadorian Highlands." *Latin America Research Review*. 29(3): 37–68.

Zárate B., Carlos G. (1993). "Cambio Ambiental y Apropiación del Espacio en la Historia de la Alta Amazonía Ecuatoriana." in Lucy Ruiz M. *Amazonía: Escenarios y Conflictos*. Quito: Abya-Yala.

Index